Marguerite Patten's
100 GREAT MENUS

Marguerite Patten's
100 GREAT MENUS

Dolphin Press

First published by Sundial Books Limited
This edition published by Treasure Press
59 Grosvenor Street
London W1

© 1973 Hennerwood Publications Limited

ISBN 0 907407 06 4

Printed in Hong Kong

This edition produced for:
Dolphin Press, 9150 S.W. 87th Ave.,
Suite 108, Miami, Florida, U.S.A.

Contents

Introduction

This is a book of complete menus for many different occasions and requirements. As you will see from the Contents on page 5, they range from Celebration Meals of all kinds to menus for the days when the housekeeping budget is at its lowest. I have also included suggestions for Slimming Meals and some that pay special attention to Health-giving Foods, so if you, or a member of your family, are over-weight or seem less fit than usual, these meals should help to solve the problems.

In many cases I have suggested dishes that are a good basis for variation, so that after you have tried the recipe as written, you can alter the flavourings, or use a different meat, fish or fruit.

I hope you enjoy using these menus and that they will provide your family and friends with pleasurable meals, while allowing you, the cook, to relax a little when it comes to the ever-present problem of 'what shall we have to eat?'.

Marguerite Patten

Aids When Planning Meals

Shopping takes a great deal of time and effort, so it is wise to have a well stocked larder, refrigerator and home freezer (if you own this modern appliance). If you choose the foods carefully you can plan menus over several days without shopping.

Your store cupboard
Naturally you will have supplies of flour, cornflour, sugars (caster for cakes, brown sugar for richer cakes, icing sugar for decorating cakes), tea and coffee, but make sure you have :–
rice – long grain for savoury dishes, such as Paella, see page 100 and to serve with various savoury dishes; round grain – for puddings.
pasta – spaghetti, etc., for quick and economical savoury dishes, see page 16.
dehydrated herbs – if you do not grow your own fresh herbs.
dehydrated vegetables – these take up little space; modern dried peas and beans do not need prolonged soaking. Dehydrated potatoes enable you to make mashed potatoes and other savoury dishes very quickly and easily. Dehydrated onion saves the bother of chopping the fresh vegetable if a little flavouring is needed.
spices and flavouring essences
sauces – such as soy, and Worcestershire.
Modern canned foods are both varied and excellent.
canned soups – choose some of the unusual ones and those that could be used for sauces.
canned meats – tongue, ham, stewed steak, pork and ham are all useful; see recipes using these on pages 18 and 22.
canned fish – sardines, tuna, salmon can all be turned into interesting dishes, see pages 16 and 18.
canned fruit – can be served by itself or it can form part of an interesting dessert, see pages 20, 26 and 47.
canned cream and/or evaporated milk and
dehydrated milk – ensure you are never short of these valuable foods.
root vegetables – store well in a cool place; use them in rotation, otherwise potatoes become green and carrots shrivel up.
citrus fruits keep well in a cool place.

Your refrigerator
Use your refrigerator in a sensible manner; do not expect perishable foods to keep more than a few days, check that you use items such as butter in the order in which it was purchased. It is all too easy to bring in fresh supplies, use these first and still have old stocks. Naturally you will use much of your refrigerator space for meat and fish, and for left-over foods you plan to use up within a day or two, but in addition check you have :–
butter, margarine and other fats – these keep well. Oil does not need keeping in the refrigerator, it can be stored in a cupboard.
cheese – the true strong cooking cheese, Parmesan – need not be stored in the refrigerator; it can be purchased ready-grated or grate your own and keep in a screw-topped container. Store Gruyère, Cheddar and hard cheeses in the refrigerator; cover well, to prevent drying. Never waste dry pieces of Cheddar or similar cheese, grate and use in cooking. Brie, Camembert and Stilton are better if kept in a cupboard at room temperature.
fresh parsley and other herbs and salad ingredients – these keep well in covered containers in the refrigerator.
bacon – wrap or buy in polythene bags (note the date by which the bacon must be used). Keep adequate stocks so you can use this for quick savoury dishes, see page 16.

Your home freezer
Use this as a supermarket in your own home. Keep a clear record of just *what* is in the cabinet and where it has been placed and label packages of food clearly, so there is no problem of finding them, and so you can keep a good idea of your 'stock'. In addition to making up dishes to keep in the freezer for emergencies, these are some of the useful frozen foods to store:
vegetables and fruits – excellent for all purposes.
meat – steaks, chops and smaller pieces of meat can be cooked from the frozen state, so can jointed raw chicken. Whole poultry and joints should be defrosted before using.
fish – ready-coated for frying, shell fish, etc.
bread, cakes, scones – sliced bread can be toasted from the frozen state and rolls need just a few minutes warming through.
ice cream – home- or commercially-made which can be bought in bulk.

Money Saving Meals

Many good foods are inexpensive to buy and you will find a selection of interesting dishes that form appetising, as well as cheap, meals in the next pages. Be selective about shopping, choose foods that are in season, for those out-of-season are always more expensive and often not at their best.

Learn about the cheaper meats, stewing steak, minced beef (excellent for meat sauces, loaves, hamburgers), neck and breast of lamb.

Choose some of the inexpensive white fish and 'dress it up' with flavoursome sauces.

Buy in larger quantities where practicable and save money that way.

All menus in this chapter serve 4–6.

GARBURE (BEAN SOUP)

**1 or 2 rashers inexpensive bacon · 1 oz. fat · 1 large onion · 1 clove garlic (optional) · 2 carrots · 1¼ pints beef or chicken stock or water and stock cubes · 1 medium-sized can haricot beans ·
Topping: chopped parsley · grated cheese**

Chop the bacon and fry lightly for a few minutes. Lift out of the pan, add the fat to the bacon fat in the pan and heat. Chop the onion, crush the garlic, if used. Fry the onion and garlic until soft, but not brown. Add the chopped or grated carrots and stock or water and stock cubes. Simmer for 15 minutes, add beans and bacon. Serve topped with parsley and cheese.

DEVILLED COD

**2½ oz. margarine or butter ·
1–2 teaspoons curry powder ·
1 teaspoon Worcestershire sauce ·
1–2 tablespoons sultanas ·**

**1 tablespoon sweet chutney · good shake pepper · pinch salt · 3 tablespoons soft breadcrumbs · 4 or 6 portions cod ·
Garnish: lemon · watercress**

Grease an ovenproof dish with ½ oz. margarine or butter. Melt the remainder, and blend with the curry powder, Worcestershire sauce, sultanas and chutney. Add the pepper and salt, mix well, then stir the breadcrumbs into the mixture. Spread over the top of the fish and bake, uncovered, for approximately 25 minutes in a moderately hot oven, 400°F., Gas Mark 6. Garnish and serve with salad.

LEMON APPLE MERINGUE PIE

**short crust pastry, made with 6 oz. flour, etc. (see page 70) · 2 really large cooking apples · grated rind and juice 1 lemon ·
4–7 oz. sugar (see method) · 2 eggs**

Line a 7–8-inch flan case with the pastry. Bake 'blind'. Meanwhile, peel, slice and cook the apples with the lemon rind and juice and 2–3 oz. sugar until a thick pulp. Beat or sieve until smooth, then add the 2 beaten egg yolks. Spoon into the pastry case. Whisk the egg whites until very stiff, then very gradually beat in 2–4 oz. sugar. Either bake for about 25–30 minutes in a very moderate oven, 325°F., Gas Mark 3, and serve hot, or bake for about 1 hour in a very slow oven, 275°F., Gas Mark 1, and serve cold. Use the larger amount of sugar if serving cold.

Garbure, Devilled Cod, Salad, Lemon Apple Meringue Pie

MENU

STEAK UPSIDE DOWN PIE
CREAMED CARROTS
LYONNAISE POTATOES
GRAPE AND ORANGE WHIP

STEAK UPSIDE DOWN PIE

2 onions · 2–3 tomatoes ·
a few mushrooms or mushroom stalks ·
2 oz. dripping ·
½ pint stock or water and a beef stock cube ·
12 oz. raw minced beef · seasoning ·
Topping: 6 oz. self-raising flour or plain flour and
1½ teaspoons baking powder · seasoning ·
2 oz. fat · 2 oz. Cheddar cheese · 1 egg yolk · milk ·
Garnish: parsley sprigs

Chop the vegetables and fry in the dripping until soft. Add the stock or water and stock cube and the minced beef. Stir until a smooth, thick mixture, season well, cook for 15 minutes only in an uncovered pan, stir from time to time. Meanwhile prepare the topping. Sieve the flour or flour and baking powder with seasoning. Rub in the fat, add the grated cheese – this is an excellent way to use stale pieces. Bind with the egg yolk and milk to make a soft rolling consistency. Form into a 7–8-inch round. Put the meat mixture into a cake tin (without a loose base) or oven-proof dish, top with the dough. Bake in the centre of a moderate oven, 350–375°F., Gas Mark 4–5, for about 50 minutes. Invert on to a hot dish and garnish with

CREAMED CARROTS

Cook and mash carrots with a knob of margarine or butter, 1–2 tablespoons top of the milk, a little grated nutmeg and plenty of seasoning. Top with chopped parsley.

LYONNAISE POTATOES

1 lb. cooked potatoes · about 8 oz. raw onions ·
2 oz. fat or dripping · chopped parsley

Slice the potatoes fairly thickly. Slice the raw onion very thinly. Heat the fat or dripping in a pan and cook the onions until nearly tender. Add the potatoes and mix well, then heat gently until pale golden. Top with chopped parsley before serving.

GRAPE AND ORANGE WHIP

2–3 very large oranges ·
1 orange flavoured jelly ·
2–3 tablespoons thick cream · 1 egg white ·
skinned de-seeded grapes ·
few whole or halved grapes

Halve the oranges carefully. Squeeze out the juice, but try to keep the orange cases intact. Measure the juice and add enough water to give just ¾ pint. Dissolve the jelly in this and allow to cool, then begin to stiffen slightly. Whisk sharply then fold in the cream and stiffly beaten egg white (left from the main dish). Put a layer of skinned de-seeded grapes at the bottom of each orange case, top with the jelly mixture and decorate with whole or halved grapes when set.

Steak Upside Down Pie with Creamed Carrots and Lyonnaise Potatoes, Grape and Orange Whip

GOLDEN CHEESE SOUP

2 oz. margarine or butter · 2 oz. flour · ½ pint milk ·
¾ pint chicken stock or water and a stock cube ·
2 carrots, grated · 4–6 oz. Cheddar cheese, grated ·
Topping: chopped parsley or watercress leaves

Heat the margarine or butter in a pan, stir in the flour and cook gently for several minutes. Gradually stir in the milk and chicken stock or water and stock cube. Bring to the boil, stir well until thickened. Add the grated carrots, cook for a few minutes only, then add the grated cheese. Heat until melted. Pour into soup cups, top with chopped parsley, or watercress.

MILANAISE KIDNEYS

2–3 onions, thinly sliced ·
about 4 large tomatoes, skinned, or canned tomatoes ·
fat for frying · approximately ¼ pint stock ·
about 7 lambs' kidneys★, halved · seasoning ·
1–2 teaspoons cornflour ·
few tablespoons extra stock or cheap red wine ·
Garnish: grilled or fried snippets of bacon
★If using pigs' kidneys, slice and use more liquid.

Fry the thinly sliced onions and the tomatoes in a little fat until soft. Add the stock and lambs' kidneys. Season well and simmer steadily in a covered pan for about 10–15 minutes. Blend the cornflour with the extra stock or wine. Stir into the mixture and continue stirring as the mixture thickens. Serve with noodles and garnish with grilled or fried snippets of bacon.

CAULIFLOWER POLANAISE

1 cauliflower · 1–2 tablespoons soft breadcrumbs ·
small knob margarine ·
1–2 tablespoons chopped parsley · 1 hard boiled egg ·

Break the cauliflower into sprigs. Cook until just tender, strain, then arrange neatly in a serving dish. Fry the breadcrumbs in the margarine, add the chopped parsley and finally the chopped hard-boiled egg. Spoon over the cauliflower just before serving.

HONEY BANANA CREAMS

3 large ripe bananas · 1 large lemon ·
2–3 tablespoons honey · ½ pint milk ·
½ oz. powdered gelatine · ¼ pint water ·
2–3 tablespoons cream ·
Topping: ice cream or cream

Mash the bananas with the lemon juice. Heat the honey in the milk, stir into the mashed bananas. Soften the gelatine in 3 tablespoons of the cold water. Simmer the lemon rind in the remainder of the water for about 5–6 minutes to extract the maximum flavour, then blend the liquid with the softened gelatine. When quite clear add to the banana mixture. Allow to cool and stiffen very slightly then fold in the lightly whipped cream. Spoon into glasses, top with ice cream or cream.

Honey Banana Creams

2–3 tablespoons chopped gherkins ·
1 teaspoon liquid from gherkins ·
1–2 teaspoons chopped fresh herbs · 1 egg ·
chicken stock
Garnish: watercress

Simmer the chicken giblets in a little water to make some stock. Blend the sausagemeat with the rest of the ingredients. To give a moist texture to the stuffing add a little giblet stock. Put the stuffing into the chicken and weigh. Allow 15 minutes per lb. and 15 minutes over in a moderately hot to hot oven, 400–425°F., Gas Mark 6–7. Cover the chicken breast with fat to keep it moist during cooking. If preferred wrap in foil, but allow 30 minutes longer cooking time and open the foil for the last 30 minutes to brown the bird. Serve with thickened gravy, from the giblet stock. If you wish to give this a slightly sweet sour flavour, add 2 teaspoons honey and a squeeze of lemon juice after it has thickened. Serve with roast potatoes and cooked corn and garnish with watercress.

MENU

**SOUFFLE EGGS
ROAST CHICKEN WITH SWEET
SOUR STUFFING
ROAST POTATOES AND CORN
APPLE AND DATE CHARLOTTE**

SOUFFLE EGGS

**4 eggs · 1 oz. butter · 2 tablespoons thin cream ·
seasoning · 2–3 oz. cooked ham or grated cheese**

Separate the egg yolks from the whites, whisk the whites until stiff. Butter individual oven-proof shallow dishes. Beat the yolks with the cream, season well, mix with tiny pieces of ham or grated cheese and fold into the whites. Put into the dishes and bake for 10 minutes towards the top of a moderately hot to hot oven, 400–425 F., Gas Mark 6–7. Serve at once.

ROAST CHICKEN WITH SWEET SOUR STUFFING

**1 × 4½ lb. roasting chicken with giblets · water ·
1 lb. sausagemeat · 2–3 tablespoons seedless raisins ·
2–3 tablespoons chopped walnuts ·**

APPLE AND DATE CHARLOTTE

**6 slices bread · margarine or butter ·
about 1 lb. cooking apples · 2–3 tablespoons sugar ·
4 oz. chopped dates · cinnamon · brown sugar**

Spread the bread with the margarine or butter, remove the crusts if wished. Cut the slices of bread into fingers. Simmer the peeled sliced apples in the minimum of water, adding the sugar. When soft add the dates and a sprinkling of powdered cinnamon to taste. Sprinkle the bottom of a pie dish with a little brown sugar. Put half the fingers of bread in the dish with the buttered side towards the sugar so it will brown and crisp. Cover with the apple mixture, then the rest of the slices of bread and butter, this time the buttered side uppermost. Sprinkle lightly with brown sugar. Bake for about 10–15 minutes, then leave in the oven when removing the chicken, but lower the heat to very moderate, 325 F., Gas Mark 3.

Above : Roast Chicken with Sweet Sour Stuffing, Roast Potatoes and Cooked Corn

Opposite page : Apple and Date Charlotte

This menu provides a buffet or formal meal for 6 people at a reasonable cost.

AVOCADO COCKTAIL

**1 grapefruit · 1 ripe avocado pear ·
2 oz. shelled prawns · little mayonnaise · lettuce**

Cut away the peel and pith from the grapefruit and remove the fruit segments. Put 6 segments on one side for garnish. Cut the remainder into small pieces and put into a basin. Halve the avocado pear, remove the stone, skin and slice the fruit. Mix with the grapefruit pieces, prawns and a little mayonnaise. Arrange a little finely shredded lettuce in individual glasses or on small dishes, top with the avocado and prawn mixture and garnish with the reserved grapefruit segments.

HAM AND MUSHROOM FLAN

**short crust pastry made with 8 oz. flour, etc.
(see page 70)
1½ oz. margarine · 1½ oz. flour · ¾ pint milk ·
6–8 oz. cooked ham · 4–6 tablespoons grated cheese ·
seasoning · 12 button mushrooms · 1 oz. butter or fat**

Make the pastry, roll out and make a 9–10-inch flan case.

Bake 'blind' until crisp and golden brown. Meanwhile make a white sauce with the margarine, flour and milk, see recipe opposite. Add the neatly diced ham, grated cheese and seasoning. Heat for a few minutes only. Fry the mushrooms in the butter or fat. Fill the *hot* pastry case with the *hot* ham mixture. Top with the cooked mushrooms and serve as soon as possible.

CUCUMBER AND TOMATO SALAD

**watercress · cucumber · tomatoes · seasoning ·
vinegar or lemon juice · chives or spring onions**

Put a layer of watercress into a shallow dish. Arrange thin slices of cucumber and tomato over this. Flavour with salt, pepper, a little vinegar or lemon juice and chopped chives or spring onions.

PEACH AND CHERRY TRIFLE

**1 pint thick custard sauce · lemon or orange rind ·
Swiss roll or sponge cake · jam ·
1–2 sliced fresh peaches or 1 medium-sized can peaches
Decoration: 1 or 2 fresh peaches · lemon juice ·
¼ pint thick cream, lightly whipped ·
glacé or fresh cherries**

Make the custard sauce as the instructions on the can, but put thin strips of lemon or orange rind into the milk and remove when the custard has thickened. Arrange 6 slices of Swiss roll or sponge cake, split and spread with jam, in a serving dish. Top with the sliced fresh peaches (when cheap) or half the drained canned peaches. Spoon the hot custard sauce over the sponge and fruit and allow to cool. Decorate with the thinly sliced fresh peaches (dipped in lemon juice) or the remainder of the canned fruit, the whipped cream and cherries.

Peach and Cherry Trifle

Grapefruit and Melon Cocktails

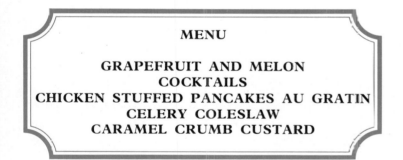

<table>
<tr><td align="center">MENU

GRAPEFRUIT AND MELON
COCKTAILS
CHICKEN STUFFED PANCAKES AU GRATIN
CELERY COLESLAW
CARAMEL CRUMB CUSTARD</td></tr>
</table>

GRAPEFRUIT AND MELON COCKTAILS

This is an excellent way of using part of a melon.

**2 oz. sugar · $\frac{1}{4}$ pint water · 1 tablespoon sherry
little ground ginger · 2 large grapefruit, halved ·
$\frac{1}{2}$ small melon**

Make a syrup by boiling together the sugar and water. Flavour with the sherry and ginger. Take the segments from the grapefruit, mix with the diced melon. Put into glasses. Spoon over the syrup and chill.

CHICKEN STUFFED PANCAKES AU GRATIN

This is a good way to use left-over pieces of chicken.

**8–12 pancakes (see page 16) · $\frac{3}{4}$ pint white sauce
(see below)
small pieces cooked chicken · stuffing ·
$\frac{1}{2}$ chopped green or red pepper · little cooked corn ·
soft breadcrumbs · little grated cheese ·
little margarine or butter**

Cook the pancakes as the recipe on page 16. Make a creamy white sauce (see below), using a little chicken stock for flavouring the sauce. Mix half of this with small pieces of cooked chicken, tiny pieces of stuffing, if available, chopped green or red pepper and a little cooked corn. Fill the pancakes with this, then put into an oven-proof dish. Spoon over the remaining sauce, breadcrumbs and a little grated cheese. Top with a little margarine or butter (melted or in small pieces) and heat for about 25 minutes in a moderately hot oven, 375–400 F., Gas Mark 5–6. Serve at once.

To make white sauce: Heat $1\frac{1}{2}$ oz. margarine in a pan, stir in $1\frac{1}{2}$ oz. flour and cook for 2–3 minutes. Add $\frac{3}{4}$ pint milk, bring to the boil, stirring or whisking well until smooth. Cook until thickened, then season.

CELERY COLESLAW

**$\frac{1}{2}$ small cabbage · few sticks raw celery ·
little mayonnaise · few gherkins · few capers**

Toss the finely shredded cabbage and finely chopped celery in the mayonnaise. Add tiny pieces of chopped gherkin and a few capers.

CARAMEL CRUMB CUSTARD

**1 pint thick custard sauce · plain sponge cake ·
little fruit juice, sherry or white wine ·
cooked apples or other fresh or cooked fruit ·
caramel (see page 16)**

Make the custard sauce as the instructions on the can. Dice the sponge cake and put into individual glasses. Moisten with a very little fruit juice, sherry or white wine, then top with the sliced cooked apples or other fruit. Spoon the warm custard over the top and allow it to cool. Meanwhile make the caramel as page 16. When the sugar mixture is brown pour it on to a tin and let it set. Crush with a rolling pin and sprinkle over the top of each dessert.

MENU

SPAGHETTI WITH BACON AND ONION
FRESH FRUIT

SPAGHETTI WITH BACON AND ONION

**8 oz. spaghetti · seasoning ·
6 oz. streaky or other bacon · 3 large onions ·
chopped parsley · grated cheese**

Cook the spaghetti in seasoned boiling water until nearly tender. Chop the bacon and fry for 2–3 minutes; fry the rinds too, to extract the fat. Add the chopped or grated onions and cook steadily. Drain the spaghetti and return to the pan, add the bacon and onions and as much parsley and cheese as desired, then serve.

MENU

GRILLED COD STEAKS
WITH PARSLEY BUTTER
PEAS AND CREAMED POTATOES
CARAMELLED APPLES

GRILLED COD STEAKS

**4 cod steaks · seasoning · juice of ½ a lemon ·
1½–2 oz. butter or margarine ·
Garnish: 1 lemon · parsley**

Season the fish and flavour with the lemon juice. Melt the butter or margarine. Brush either the grid of the grill pan, or a piece of foil spread over the grid of the grill pan (this saves time in washing up) with butter or margarine. Put the fish on the grid or foil, brush with butter or margarine and grill quickly for 2–3 minutes. Turn and grill quickly for the same time on the other side, then lower the heat and cook for a few more minutes until the cod is tender. Lift on to a hot dish, top with the parsley butter (see below) and garnish with sliced lemon and parsley.

PARSLEY BUTTER

Cream 1½–2 oz. butter or margarine with seasoning, the finely grated rind and juice of ½ lemon and 1–2 tablespoons chopped parsley. Cut into 4 neat slices or form into 4 rounds. Chill well and put on the fish before serving.
To vary: Add 1 tablespoon chopped fresh dill or a good pinch of the dried herb in place of the parsley. Add the lemon juice as above.

CARAMELLED APPLES

**4 oz. caster or granulated sugar · ¼ pint water ·
4 dessert apples**

For the caramel sauce, put the sugar and 4 tablespoons water into a strong pan, stir until the sugar has dissolved, then boil *without stirring* until golden brown. Add the rest of the water and blend with the caramel. Peel, core and slice the apples, put into a dish, add the warm caramel then allow to cool. Turn over once or twice so the apples absorb the sauce.

MENU

TUNA PANCAKES AND
MIXED SALAD
COOKED FRUIT AND
ICE CREAM

TUNA PANCAKES

**Pancakes: 4 oz. plain flour · pinch salt · 1 egg ·
½ pint milk or milk and water · fat for frying ·
Filling: 1 medium sized can tuna · nearly ½ pint milk ·
1 oz. margarine · 1 onion · 1 oz. flour ·
2 tablespoons chopped parsley · seasoning**

Sieve the flour and salt, add the egg and liquid, then beat until a smooth batter. Heat a little fat in the pan, pour in enough batter to give a thin coating, fry for 2 minutes, turn and fry on the second side. Lift on to a heat-proof dish and top with a little filling. Keep hot in the oven and make a gâteau of pancakes and filling. To make the filling, flake the fish, add any liquid from the can to the milk. Heat the margarine and fry the chopped onion for 3–4 minutes, blend the flour and liquid and stir into the onion, continue stirring until thickened. Add the rest of the ingredients.
To vary: Add tiny pieces of lemon pulp, diced cucumber, chopped hard-boiled egg, etc. to the tuna.

MENU

SARDINE FRITTERS
CHEF'S SALAD
NEW POTATOES
FRESH FRUIT SALAD AND YOGHOURT

SARDINE FRITTERS

**1 small can sardines in oil · ½ lemon · seasoning ·
6 large slices of bread · 1 oz. butter ·
Coating: 1 egg · 2 tablespoons milk ·
For frying: 1 oz. cooking fat**

Drain, bone and mash the sardines with lemon juice and plenty of seasoning. Cut the crusts from the bread, spread with butter, do not be too generous, since sardines are a very oily fish. Sandwich the bread with the mashed sardines, cut into fingers; makes about 12 fingers. Beat the egg and milk, dip the fingers in this. Put any oil from the can of sardines into the pan plus the fat. Heat gently until the fat has melted, then fry the sardine fingers until crisp and brown on either side. Drain on absorbent paper and serve at once.
To vary: Use pilchards, either in oil or in tomato sauce, or use sardines in tomato sauce.

CHEF'S SALAD

This is not only a good picnic dish, see page 68, but an economical one too. Serve with canned or freshly cooked new potatoes.

Spaghetti with Bacon and Onion

Time Saving Menus

The very large range of convenience foods available means that good meals, interesting meals and nutritious meals can be prepared within minutes.
Canned Foods Meat, fish, fruit and vegetables all add variety to a menu and the food needs little, if any, heating.
Frozen Foods These have caused a mild 'revolution' in our kitchens.
Fresh 'Convenience Foods' Cooked meats, cheese, milk, bread and many fruits and vegetables can be termed 'convenience foods', for they can provide the basis of speedy and interesting meals.
All menus in this chapter serve 4.

MENU

DANISH KEBABS
WITH MUSTARD SAUCE
AND GREEN SALAD
ORANGE CONDE
CHEESE WAFERS

DANISH KEBABS WITH MUSTARD SAUCE

1 small can luncheon meat or ham and pork ·
1 small can Frankfurters · 1 small can or tube pâté ·
4–8 firm tomatoes · 1 oz. margarine or butter ·
Sauce: 1 small can chicken soup* ·
French or English mustard

Cut the meat into 1½-inch cubes. If the Frankfurters are large, halve. Split them carefully, spread with a little pâté, and sandwich together again. Quarter the tomatoes. Put the food on to 4 long or 8 smaller metal skewers. Brush with melted margarine or butter and heat under the grill. Heat the chicken soup and flavour with a generous amount of French or English mustard. Serve as a sauce with the kebabs.

ORANGE CONDE

3 or 4 oranges · 1 medium-sized can creamed rice ·
2–3 tablespoons marmalade, jam or red currant jelly

Cut the peel from the oranges, slice the fruit neatly. Blend some of the fruit with the rice. Spoon into 4 individual dishes. Heat the marmalade, jam or jelly. Arrange the rest of the oranges on the rice and top with the hot preserve.

CHEESE WAFERS

8 ice cream wafer biscuits ·
4 thin slices processed or Cheddar cheese, or 1–2 oz.
cream cheese · ½ oz. butter or margarine

Sandwich the wafers together with the cheese slices or cream cheese. Put on to a baking tray, brush with melted butter or margarine and heat for about 3 minutes only in a hot oven, 425°F., Gas Mark 7.

MENU

CHICKEN BORSHCH
SARDINES NIÇOISE
CHEESE, BISCUITS, BUTTER
CELERY AND/OR FRESH FRUIT

CHICKEN BORSHCH

1 medium-sized can chicken soup ·
little top of the milk or thin cream ·
liquid from a small can beetroot · chopped parsley

Tip the soup into a pan and heat. Add a little top of the milk or thin cream and the beetroot liquid. Garnish with chopped parsley.

SARDINES NIÇOISE

1 small can tomatoes · seasoning ·
1 medium-sized can sardines ·
4 crumpets or slices of bread · butter ·
anchovy fillets · black olives

Tip the tomatoes into a pan, add seasoning and simmer until a *thick* pulp. Mash the sardines, season lightly. Toast the crumpets or slices of bread. Butter, then spread with the sardines. Heat under the grill for a few minutes. Top with the tomato pulp, anchovy fillets and black olives.

CELERY CHEESE BISCUITS

These are useful to have in a tin.

Cream 3 oz. butter, ½–1 teaspoon celery salt, a shake of pepper, 1 oz. grated Parmesan cheese and 3 oz. self-raising flour or plain flour with 1 teaspoon baking powder. Form into 12–15 balls and put on 2 greased and floured baking sheets. Bake for 15 minutes in the centre of a very moderate oven, 325–350°F., Gas Mark 3–4. Cool on the baking sheets.

Chicken Borshch, Sardines Niçoise,
Cheese, Fresh Fruit

Queensland Cocktail

QUEENSLAND COCKTAIL

**1 large or 2 small avocado pears · mayonnaise ·
1 small can crab meat · 1 green pepper · lettuce ·
1 lemon**

Halve the avocado pear or pears, remove skin and dice the flesh. Blend with mayonnaise immediately so the pear does not discolour. Mix with the crab meat and diced green pepper. Shred part of a lettuce finely, put at the bottom of 4 glasses. Top with the avocado mixture. Quarter the lemon and put a section on top of each glass. Serve with a teaspoon.
To vary: Use fresh crab or other cooked shell fish.

CURRIED HARD BOILED EGGS

**4–8 eggs* · 1 fairly large can mulligatawny soup ·
little curry powder (optional) ·
1–2 teaspoons chutney · 1 tablespoon raisins ·
1 tablespoon desiccated coconut ·
1 large can mixed vegetables**
*depending upon your appetite

Put the eggs on to hard boil. Meanwhile heat the soup, add a little curry powder if wished (the soup already has a curry

taste), the chutney, raisins, coconut and well drained mixed vegetables. Crack the hard-boiled eggs, remove the shells. Put the eggs into a heated dish, pour over the curried mixture. Serve with bread and butter, creamed dehydrated potatoes or long grain rice. To make the curry more interesting, serve chutney, nuts, sliced bananas and/or orange in individual dishes.
To vary: It is possible to buy canned curry sauce; use this instead of the soup.
Use chicken soup instead of mulligatawny.
Use flaked canned tuna instead of eggs.
Use frozen mixed vegetables and simmer in the soup until tender.
Use dehydrated vegetables and cook as the directions on the packet, then add to the soup.

MOCK SAVARIN

**1 medium-sized can of fruit* · 2 tablespoons rum ·
small plain Madeira cake or sponge**
*preferably mangoes, apricots, peaches or pineapple or a mixture of these fruits

Open the can of fruit, pour $\frac{1}{4}$ pint of the syrup into a saucepan. Add the rum and heat. Put the cake or sponge on a dish, spoon the syrup over this. Top with the canned fruit.
To vary: Use fresh instead of canned fruit and make the syrup with $\frac{1}{4}$ pint water and 2 oz. sugar. Honey or golden syrup could be used instead of sugar. Add the rum as above.
Add a few drops of rum essence in place of rum.
Use slices of left over plain sponge or fruit cake in place of the whole sponge.
Use a liqueur, i.e. Cointreau or Curaçao in place of the rum.

Cutlets Indienne with Sauté Potatoes

MENU

**CREAM OF WATERCRESS SOUP
CUTLETS INDIENNE WITH
SAUTE POTATOES AND
TOMATOES
CARDINAL PEACHES**

CREAM OF WATERCRESS SOUP

**2 oz. margarine · 2 oz. flour · ½ pint milk ·
½ pint chicken stock or water and 1 chicken stock cube
1 lemon · 1 large bunch watercress ·
¼ pint thin cream · seasoning**

Make a sauce with the margarine, flour, milk and stock or water and stock cube (see page 15). Add the finely grated rind of the lemon and the stalks of the watercress (tied together with cotton) if you like a fairly hot flavour. Simmer for 5–6 minutes, then remove the watercress stalks. Add a little lemon juice, the cream and the finely chopped watercress leaves. Season well and heat gently.

CUTLETS INDIENNE

**1 oz. margarine · 1–2 teaspoons curry powder ·
shake cayenne pepper · 8 lamb cutlets
Garnish: watercress or parsley**

Melt the margarine, add the curry powder and pepper. Brush the cutlets with the mixture and grill as usual. Garnish with watercress or parsley.

CARDINAL PEACHES

**2 tablespoons red currant jelly · 1 oz. sugar ·
½ pint water · 4 firm, but ripe peaches**

Put the jelly, sugar and water into a frying or large shallow pan. Heat until the jelly melts. Skin and halve the peaches, put into the syrup and simmer gently for 5 minutes.

MENU

**TONGUE PATE
CHICKEN BASQUE WITH FRIED
POTATOES AND BROCCOLI
CHEESE AND BISCUITS**

TONGUE PATE

**3 oz. butter · 1 clove garlic · 1–2 tablespoons brandy ·
small can or 6 oz. cooked tongue · seasoning**

Cream the butter and crushed garlic. Blend in the brandy, then the finely chopped tongue and seasoning. Serve with toast.

CHICKEN BASQUE

**1 lb. tomatoes, skinned · 1 onion · ¼ pint stock ·
2 oz. fat · 4 joints frying chicken ·
2 tablespoons chopped parsley**

Chop the tomatoes and onion and simmer with the stock. Meanwhile heat the fat and fry the chicken until just golden. Add to the purée and simmer for 15 minutes. Top with parsley.

CORN SCRAMBLE

1 oz. margarine · 2 tablespoons top of the milk ·
1 small can sweet corn · 4 eggs · seasoning

Heat the margarine in a pan with the milk. Add the drained corn and heat. Beat the eggs with seasoning. Add to the pan and scramble lightly, serve with rolls.

SPEEDY GRILL

1 small can Frankfurters ·
12 oz. can corned beef or chopped pork or ham ·
1 oz. melted margarine · canned mushrooms or tomatoes

Brush the drained sausages and sliced meat with melted margarine and cook under the grill for a few minutes. Serve with canned heated mushrooms or tomatoes.

To vary: Buy fresh sausages or bacon and combine these ingredients with sliced canned ham, or buy frozen Hamburgers which cook very quickly.

CORNFLAKE FLAN

2 oz. butter or margarine · 2 oz. caster sugar ·
2 teaspoons golden syrup ·
4 oz. cornflakes, slightly crushed · canned fruit ·
cream (optional)

Cream the butter or margarine, sugar and golden syrup. Add the cornflakes. Form into a flan shape. Either set in a cool place for a short time or brown for 10 minutes in a very moderate oven, 325°F., Gas Mark 3. Fill with fruit and decorate with cream if liked.

SPEEDY MOUSSAKA

2–3 potatoes · 2–3 onions ·
2–3 oz. margarine or dripping ·
1 large can stewed steak ·
1 oz. flour or ½ oz. cornflour · ½ pint milk ·
1 oz. margarine or butter · seasoning ·
2–3 oz. grated Cheddar cheese · grated nutmeg

Peel and grate the potatoes and onions. Heat the margarine or dripping in a frying pan. Cook the potatoes and onions *steadily* until just tender. This takes about 8 minutes. Tip the stewed steak into the frying pan and blend with the vegetables. Heat thoroughly. Meanwhile make a white sauce by the speedy method, i.e. blend the flour or cornflour with the milk. Tip into a saucepan with the margarine or butter and stir until thickened. Season well, add the grated cheese and heat gently until melted. Put the meat and vegetables into a heated shallow casserole. Top with the sauce and a little grated nutmeg and serve at once. Serve with a green vegetable.

Note: Use less grated Parmesan cheese. This is an excellent 'stand-by' in the cupboard as it keeps well in drums.

To vary: Add a finely sliced or diced aubergine to the potatoes and onions in the frying pan. You will need a little more margarine or dripping.

COCONUT GATEAU

2 oz. butter · 2 oz. brown sugar ·
finely grated rind and juice of 1 lemon ·
2–3 tablespoons desiccated coconut ·
7-inch sponge cake · little jam

Cream the butter and brown sugar with the lemon rind and juice. Add the coconut. Split the sponge cake across the centre. If not spread with jam, cover the bottom half with a little jam then half the coconut mixture. Put the two halves together again. Spread the top of the sponge with the rest of the coconut mixture and brown under a low grill. Serve warm or cold with a jam sauce, made by heating a little jam.

MUSHROOMS A LA GRECQUE

1 tablespoon oil · juice 1 lemon · seasoning ·
¼ pint white wine ·
1 medium-sized can or 8 oz. mushrooms

Put all the ingredients into a pan. Let them stand for about an hour if possible, although you can cook the dish immediately. Simmer gently for 10 minutes. Serve with fresh rolls and butter.

LIVER, SWEET AND SOUR

1 lb. lamb's liver · 2 oz. butter · ¼ pint stock ·
1–2 tablespoons chutney · 1 oz. raisins ·
½ tablespoon vinegar · seasoning

Cut the liver into narrow strips. Fry in the hot butter for 3 minutes only, then add the rest of the ingredients and simmer gently for 6–8 minutes.

ORANGE PANCAKES

pancake batter made with 4 oz. flour, etc. (see page 16) ·
3 oranges · fat for frying · little sugar

Make the pancake batter as the recipe on page 16, but add the very finely grated rind of the 3 oranges. Cook the pancakes in the hot fat, then fill with sliced oranges. Roll up, dust with sugar and decorate with orange slices then serve.

Mushrooms à la Grecque, Liver, Sweet and Sour with Rice and Peas, Orange Pancakes

MENU

SALMON A LA KING
WITH GREEN SALAD
APRICOT OMELETTE

SALMON A LA KING

**1 green pepper · 1 small onion, chopped · 2 oz. butter ·
2 oz. flour · ¾ pint milk · 1 small can sweet corn ·
1 lemon · 1 × 12 oz. can pink salmon · 4 slices of bread**

Dice the flesh of the pepper, discarding the core and seeds. Simmer for 5 minutes in water, drain. Toss the onion in the hot butter for 5 minutes, stir in the flour, then blend in the milk. Bring to the boil, and stir until thickened. Tip in the sweet corn and liquid from the can. Add the finely grated lemon rind and juice from half the lemon, the flaked salmon and any liquid from the can (remove any skin and bones). Heat without boiling. Serve garnished with crisp toast and lemon.

APRICOT OMELETTE

**6 eggs · 1½ oz. sieved icing sugar ·
2 tablespoons thin cream · 2 oz. butter ·
1 small can apricots**

Separate the egg yolks and the whites. Beat the yolks with ½ oz. sugar and the cream. Fold in the stiffly whisked egg whites. Heat the butter in a good-sized omelette pan and pour in the mixture. Allow to set for 2 minutes, move the pan under the grill, with the heat turned to medium and, continue

Paprika Mushrooms, Chicken Fricassée with Crumbed Potatoes and Garlic Beans, Coffee Pear Alaska

cooking until just firm. Meanwhile heat the apricots. Cover the omelette with half the apricots, fold and tip on to a hot dish. Top with the rest of the sugar. Mark lines on top with a heated skewer (this makes a caramel effect). Serve the rest of the apricots plus a little syrup round the omelette.

MENU

PAPRIKA MUSHROOMS
CHICKEN FRICASSEE
WITH CRUMBED POTATOES
AND GARLIC BEANS
COFFEE PEAR ALASKA

PAPRIKA MUSHROOMS

**1 small can cream · 1–2 teaspoons paprika ·
few drops vinegar · seasoning ·
1 small can button mushrooms · toast or fried bread ·
Garnish: chopped parsley**

Blend the cream, paprika and vinegar. Season well. Heat the mushrooms, drain, put on rounds of toast or fried bread. Heat the cream mixture for 1–2 minutes only. Spoon over the mushrooms and top with parsley.

CHICKEN FRICASSEE

**1 cooked chicken · 1 large can asparagus soup ·
½–1 chicken stock cube · nearly ¼ pint boiling water ·
Garnish: triangles of toast · watercress**

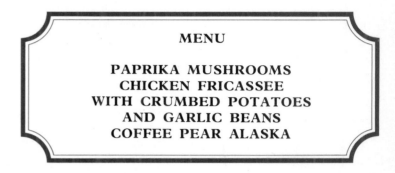

Cut the chicken into neat pieces. Remove the skin if wished. Tip the soup into a large saucepan or a deep frying pan. Blend the stock cube with the boiling water. Add to the soup, stir over a gentle heat until a smooth fairly thin mixture. Put in the chicken pieces. Heat gently, without covering the pan, for 10 minutes. The sauce should then be the right consistency. Garnish with toast and watercress.

CRUMBED POTATOES

1 large can new potatoes · 1½–2 oz. butter or margarine · 2–3 tablespoons crisp breadcrumbs (raspings)

Heat the potatoes in a pan. Drain thoroughly. Melt the butter or margarine in the saucepan, add the breadcrumbs. Put in the potatoes and turn until coated.

GARLIC BEANS

1 lb. canned, frozen or dehydrated green beans · 1 oz. butter or margarine · 1 clove garlic

Heat or cook the beans. Drain well. Heat the butter or margarine in the pan. Add the crushed garlic. Put in the beans and blend well.

COFFEE PEAR ALASKA

1 block very firm coffee ice cream · 2 or 3 pears · 4 or 5 egg whites · 4–6 oz. caster sugar

Put the ice cream on an oven-proof serving dish, or plate. Peel, core and quarter the pears, arrange round the ice cream. Whip the egg whites until *very stiff*. Gradually whisk in 2–3 oz. caster sugar, then fold in another 2–3 oz. sugar. Pile or pipe over the ice cream and fruit. Brown for 3–5 minutes in a very hot oven, 475°F, Gas Mark 8–9. This dessert can be 'kept waiting' after cooking for 15–20 minutes without spoiling.

MENU

CORNED BEEF PATTIES WITH HERBED POTATOES AND FRIED TOMATOES MUSHROOMS ON TOAST

CORNED BEEF PATTIES

about 1½ lb. cooked potatoes or equivalent in dehydrated potatoes · 3 oz. margarine · 12 oz. corned beef · 1 tablespoon grated onion · 1 egg · seasoning · Coating: 1 egg · 2 oz. crisp breadcrumbs · Herbed potatoes: 3–4 tablespoons milk · 1 tablespoon mixed chopped fresh herbs

Mash fresh potatoes or make up the dehydrated potatoes as the instructions on the packet. Add 1 oz. of the margarine. Take out about 8 oz. potatoes, mix with the flaked corned beef, onion, egg and seasoning. Form into 8 flat cakes, coat with beaten egg and crisp breadcrumbs and fry in the remaining 2 oz. margarine until crisp and brown. Drain on absorbent paper. Meanwhile blend the milk and herbs with the remaining potatoes. Arrange the patties on a hot dish in a border of herbed potatoes and fried tomatoes.

Cold Weather Menus

Once it was felt that the ideal fare for a winter's day was to start with a large filling breakfast, to have a really 'warming' main mid-day meal, perhaps soup, followed by a plate piled high with meat in some form, plenty of potatoes and other vegetables and to end the meal with a good 'old fashioned' pudding and cheese. This would probably be repeated with a similar type of menu in the evening. All this may sound sensible and wise for 'keeping out the cold', but it is not the perfect choice for wintry months. The menus in this chapter show the sort of foods you should eat in winter.

All menus in this chapter serve 4 unless stated otherwise.

MENU

**SPEEDY BORSHCH
SWEET AND SOUR HAM WITH
CRISP TOPPED NOODLES
GREEN BEANS AND
TOMATOES
CHERRY GRAPEFRUIT ALASKA**

This very satisfying meal can be prepared and cooked within a very short period.

SPEEDY BORSHCH

**1 medium-sized onion · small knob fat ·
1½ pints canned or home-made consommé,
or beef stock · seasoning, including garlic salt ·
1 large cooked beetroot ·
Topping: little yoghourt or soured or fresh cream ·
chopped parsley**

Peel and grate or chop the onion and toss it in the fat, until softened, but not brown. Add the consommé or beef stock and heat thoroughly. Season well. Cut the beetroot into thin strips or grate this, add to the soup and warm through. Spoon into individual soup bowls, top with the yoghourt or cream and chopped parsley.

SWEET AND SOUR HAM

**1½ oz. butter or margarine · 1 oz. brown sugar ·
3 tablespoons brown or white vinegar ·
3 tablespoons red currant or apple jelly ·
1–2 teaspoons made mustard · good shake pepper ·
4 slices cooked ham, about ¼–½-inch thick**

Put the butter or margarine, brown sugar, vinegar and red currant or apple jelly into a frying pan, stir over a gentle heat until the mixture forms a smooth sauce. Add the mustard and pepper; a little salt can be added if the ham is mild in flavour. Put in the slices of ham and heat gently.
To vary: Add a few drops of Worcestershire sauce or Tabasco sauce.

CRISP TOPPED NOODLES

**8 oz. noodles · salt · small knob butter or margarine ·
2 oz. breadcrumbs · 1–2 oz. grated cheese**

Cook the noodles in boiling salted water, strain. Toss in the butter or margarine and put in a heat-proof dish. Top with the breadcrumbs and cheese. Brown for a few minutes only in the oven or under the grill. Serve the slices of ham on this and spoon the sauce over the top.
To vary: Use spaghetti, macaroni on pasta shapes instead of noodles.

GREEN BEANS AND TOMATOES

**1 lb. frozen, fresh or canned green beans ·
3–4 tomatoes · seasoning**

Cook frozen or fresh green beans or heat canned beans. Strain, put into a pan with the skinned, thickly sliced tomatoes and seasoning. Heat for a few minutes only and serve.
To vary: Add a chopped onion to the pan and fry for 5 minutes in 1 oz. butter or margarine, then add the tomatoes and beans.
Add chopped herbs, parsley, thyme or chives to the pan with the tomatoes.

CHERRY GRAPEFRUIT ALASKA

**2 good-sized grapefruit · 1 small can black cherries ·
sugar to taste · ice cream · 3 egg whites ·
4 oz. caster sugar**

Halve the grapefruit, remove the segments of fruit. Discard pith, skin and pips. Put the grapefruit pieces back into the cases, together with some of the cherries. Sweeten to taste. Put a spoonful of ice cream over the fruit. Whisk the egg whites until very stiff, then gradually whisk in the caster sugar. Pile over the ice cream and fruit and decorate with a few well drained cherries. Heat for 4–5 minutes in a very hot oven
To vary: Use halved and de-seeded grapes in place of the cherries.

Speedy Borshch, Sweet and Sour Ham with Crisp Topped Noodles and Green Beans and Tomatoes, Cherry Grapefruit Alaska

MENU

CRAB AND EGG TARTLETS
LIVER SOUFFLE WITH
GREEN SALAD
APPLE PAN DOWDY

CRAB AND EGG TARTLETS

**short crust pastry made with 4 oz. flour, etc.
(see page 70) · 1 oz. butter · seasoning · 3 eggs ·
1 small can crab meat
Garnish: watercress or parsley**

Make the pastry, roll out very thinly and line 8 small patty
tins. Bake 'blind' in a hot oven, 425°F, Gas Mark 7, until crisp
and golden brown. Arrange on a dish and keep warm. Heat
the butter and scramble the well seasoned eggs blended with
the flaked crab meat. When lightly set, pile into the pastry
cases. Garnish with watercress or parsley and serve as soon as
possible.
Note: The tartlet cases can be made in advance and heated
through in a moderate oven for 5–10 minutes.
To vary: Use any other freshly cooked or canned shell fish;
chop prawns or shrimps finely.

LIVER SOUFFLE

**1 oz. butter or margarine · 1 oz. flour · $\frac{1}{4}$ pint milk ·
12 oz. minced raw lamb's or calf's liver · seasoning ·
pinch sugar · 3 egg yolks · 4 egg whites**

Make a thick sauce with the butter or margarine, flour and
milk. Add the liver, season well and add the sugar. Beat in the
egg yolks then fold in the stiffly whisked egg whites. Put into a
lightly greased 7-inch soufflé dish. Bake in the centre of a
moderate oven, 350–375°F., Gas Mark 4–5, for 35 minutes or
until lightly set.

APPLE PAN DOWDY

**3 good-sized cooking apples ·
1–2 tablespoons brown sugar ·
1–2 tablespoons golden syrup · grated nutmeg ·
ground cinnamon ·
4 oz. self-raising flour or plain flour and 1 level
teaspoon baking powder ·
pinch salt · 2 oz. sugar · 1 egg · 4 tablespoons milk ·
2 oz. melted butter or margarine · little sugar**

Peel and slice the apples. Put into a greased 1$\frac{1}{2}$-pint pie dish
with the brown sugar, syrup and a sprinkling of grated nutmeg and ground cinnamon. Do not add any water. Cover the
dish with foil and bake in the centre of a moderate oven for
about 15–20 minutes until the apples are nearly soft. Mean-

Apple Pan Dowdy

while make a thick batter mixture by blending the flour, salt, sugar, egg, milk and melted butter or margarine. Spoon the mixture over the apples, sprinkle lightly with sugar and bake in the centre of a moderate oven for 30–35 minutes. Turn the pudding upside-down on to a dish, serve with cream, brandy butter or vanilla-flavoured sauce (made as the rum sauce on page 33 but using ½–1 teaspoon vanilla essence instead of rum).

MENU

**SPICED ORANGE JUICE
BEEF GOULASH WITH
RED CABBAGE
CHEESE AND BISCUITS WITH
CELERY AND/OR CHICORY**

SPICED ORANGE JUICE

**1 pint fresh or canned orange juice ·
4 cinnamon sticks · grated nutmeg**

This is not only refreshing, but as warming as hot soup. Heat the orange juice and as it heats infuse a stick of cinnamon in this. Pour into hot glasses, top with grated nutmeg and put a cinnamon stick into each glass if liked.

BEEF GOULASH

**1¼ lb. chuck beef · 2–3 onions ·
2 oz. butter or dripping · ½ pint stock ·
2–3 teaspoons paprika ·
1 lb. skinned chopped tomatoes · seasoning ·
1 lb. potatoes (optional)
Garnish: yoghourt (optional) · chopped parsley**

Dice the meat, peel and slice the onions and toss the meat and onions in the hot butter or dripping. Blend the stock and paprika, add to the pan with the tomatoes and seasoning. Simmer gently for 1¾ hours, then add the potatoes, if using, and continue cooking for a further 45 minutes. Serve topped with yoghourt if wished, and parsley.

RED CABBAGE

**1 small red cabbage · salt ·
knob butter or margarine ·
few caraway seeds (optional)**
Shred the cabbage and cook in salted water, strain, add the butter. Flavour with caraway seeds, if wished.

CHEESE BOARD

Select a good variety of cheeses, i.e. a hard cheese such as Cheddar or Cheshire, a soft cheese with 'bite' like Camembert or Brie, a delicate cheese, Bel Paese, for example or a flavoured cream cheese.

Spiced Orange Juice, Beef Goulash with Red Cabbage, Cheese and Biscuits

MENU

LEMON TOMATO COCKTAIL
MEXICAN MACARONI
WITH SPINACH
COMPOTE OF FRUIT AND
CREAM

MENU

CHEESE STUFFED MUSHROOMS
CHICKEN HOT-POT AND
BROCCOLI
CARAMEL TOPPED RICE PUDDING
WITH GINGER PEARS

LEMON TOMATO COCKTAIL

This makes a good warming start to the meal without being too filling.

Heat 1 pint tomato juice with the juice of 1 lemon, a shake of pepper, a pinch of grated nutmeg and a shake of celery salt.

Mexican Macaroni

MEXICAN MACARONI

**Cheese sauce: 1 oz. margarine · 1 oz. flour ·
½ pint milk · 4 oz. grated cheese · seasoning ·
pinch cayenne pepper · (or use a packet of cheese
sauce mix with ½ pint milk) ·
4 oz. macaroni · 1–2 teaspoons made mustard ·
8 Frankfurter sausages ·
4–6 oz. cooked frozen, fresh or canned peas**

Make the sauce with the margarine, flour and milk. When thickened add the cheese and seasoning together with the cayenne pepper. Do not *boil* after adding the cheese, otherwise the sauce will curdle (separate). Alternatively make up the cheese sauce following the instructions on the packet. Meanwhile boil the macaroni in salted water, drain then add to the cheese sauce with enough mustard to give a fairly hot flavour. Chop the Frankfurter sausages, add to the sauce with the well-drained peas. Heat gently, then serve.

COMPOTE OF FRUIT

¼ pint water · 2 oz. sugar · about 1 lb. fresh fruit

Put the water and sugar into a saucepan, stir until the sugar has dissolved then add the prepared fruit and simmer gently until the fruit is tender.

CHEESE STUFFED MUSHROOMS

**16 large mushrooms · 2 egg yolks ·
3 tablespoons soft breadcrumbs ·
3 tablespoons grated Gruyère or Cheddar cheese ·
seasoning · little cooked ham (optional) ·
To coat: 1 egg yolk · 2 oz. crisp breadcrumbs ·
fat for frying ·**

Remove the mushroom stalks, wash and chop these. Skin the mushroom caps, wash and dry. Blend the egg yolks with the breadcrumbs, cheese and seasoning. Add the mushroom stalks to this mixture and small strips of cooked ham can also be included. Spread over 8 mushrooms, then cover with the rest of the mushrooms. Dip in the egg yolk (beaten lightly and blended with a little water), coat in crumbs, then fry in hot shallow fat until brown on one side, turn and brown on the second side. If lightly cooked these may be warmed gently in the oven or kept hot for a short time.

CHICKEN HOT-POT

**1 lb. potatoes · 12 oz. onions · 8–12 oz. tomatoes ·
seasoning · 4 chicken joints · about ¼ pint stock ·
chopped fresh or dried rosemary · margarine ·**

Put a layer of peeled thinly sliced potatoes into a casserole, cover with a layer of very thinly sliced onions and thickly sliced skinned tomatoes. Season each layer well. Put the chicken joints over the vegetables, add well seasoned stock, a light sprinkling of rosemary, then a layer of tomatoes, onions, and a topping of potato slices. Season well, put small pieces of margarine over the potatoes. Cover the casserole and cook near the centre of a very moderate oven, 325–350°F., Gas Mark 3–4, for approximately 1¼–1½ hours. Remove the lid for the last 20–30 minutes if wished, to brown the potatoes.

CARAMEL TOPPED RICE PUDDING

**2 tablespoons round grain rice ·
1–2 tablespoons sugar · 1 pint milk ·
Topping: brown sugar**

Put the rice into a pie dish or oven-proof dish. Add the sugar and milk. Bake in the coolest part of the oven for about 1 hour. Remove the dish from the oven, top with a layer of brown sugar and return to the oven for about 20–25 minutes, lowering the heat to slow, to allow the topping to caramelise.

GINGER PEARS

4 firm pears · ¾ pint ginger ale or ginger beer

Peel and halve the pears. Put into a casserole and cover with ginger ale or ginger beer. Put a lid on the casserole and bake for about 1 hour in the coolest part of the oven.

Chicken Hot-Pot

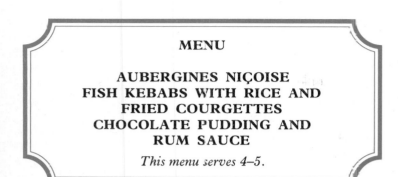

MENU

AUBERGINES NIÇOISE
FISH KEBABS WITH RICE AND
FRIED COURGETTES
CHOCOLATE PUDDING AND
RUM SAUCE

This menu serves 4–5.

AUBERGINES NIÇOISE

**2 medium-sized aubergines · seasoning ·
1–2 cloves garlic · 1 large onion · 1 tablespoon oil ·
1 oz. butter · 4–5 large tomatoes ·
Topping: chopped parsley**

Wash and dry the aubergines, slice thinly, but do not peel. Sprinkle lightly with salt and leave for about 15–20 minutes. This minimises the slightly bitter taste of the vegetable. Crush the garlic, chop the onion. Heat the oil and butter in a saucepan. Fry the garlic and onion gently for a few minutes, then add the skinned, chopped tomatoes. Simmer gently until the tomatoes become a purée. Add the aubergine slices and season well. Mix with the tomato purée, put a lid on the pan, and simmer steadily for 45–50 minutes. Serve hot topped with chopped parsley.

FISH KEBABS

**1¼–1½ lb. firm-fleshed white fish, e.g. cod, fresh
haddock or hake · about 24 small mushrooms ·
1 red pepper · 1 green pepper ·
4 oz. butter or margarine · juice 1 large lemon ·
seasoning · few drops chilli sauce ·
1 tablespoon chopped parsley ·
To serve: boiled rice**

Cut the fish into 1½-inch cubes, remove skin or bones. Wash and dry the mushrooms, cut the flesh of the red and green pepper into squares. Put the fish, mushrooms and pepper on to 4 or 5 metal skewers. Heat the butter or margarine, the lemon juice, seasoning and chilli sauce. Brush the fish and vegetables with some of the mixture. Grill quickly, turning several times, until cooked. Serve on boiled rice. Heat the remaining butter mixture, add the chopped parsley and spoon over the kebabs.

FRIED COURGETTES

**1 lb. courgettes · seasoning · 1 oz. flour ·
shallow or deep fat for frying**

Wash, dry and cut courgettes into ¼–½-inch slices. Coat in well seasoned flour and fry until crisp and golden brown. Drain on absorbent paper before serving.

CHOCOLATE PUDDING WITH RUM SAUCE

**2 oz. plain chocolate · few drops vanilla essence ·
2 oz. butter or margarine · 3–4 oz. caster sugar ·
2 eggs ·
6 oz. self-raising flour or plain flour and
1½ teaspoons baking powder · 6 tablespoons milk**

*Aubergines Niçoise, Fish Kebabs with Rice and Fried
Courgettes, Chocolate Pudding and Rum Sauce*

Put the chocolate, vanilla essence and butter or margarine into a basin, melt over a pan of hot water. Remove the basin from the pan and cool the chocolate mixture slightly. Add the sugar and blend thoroughly. Beat in the eggs then the flour and milk. Grease and flour a 2-pint basin, put in the mixture, cover and steam for 1 hour. Turn out and serve with a rum sauce.

RUM SAUCE

**2 tablespoons cornflour · ½ pint milk ·
2 tablespoons sugar · 1–2 tablespoons rum**

Blend the cornflour with the milk. Put into a saucepan with the sugar and heat, stirring well, until thickened. Add rum to taste.

To vary: Use 1–2 tablespoons brandy in place of the rum.

MENU

SMOKED TROUT WITH HORSERADISH
SAUCE
MOROCCAN LAMB WITH NOODLES
AND BRAISED CELERY
MUSHROOMS ON TOAST

MOROCCAN LAMB

**8 small or 4 large lamb chops · 12 cooked prunes ·
¼ pint syrup from cooking the prunes · ¼ pint water ·
pinch turmeric · ½–1 tablespoon sugar or honey ·
2 onions · seasoning**

Put the chops and prunes into a shallow casserole. Heat the prune syrup, water, turmeric, sugar or honey with the finely chopped onions and seasoning. Pour over the lamb and prunes. If the liquid does not quite cover the meat and prunes add a little more hot water or prune juice, but do not use too much liquid. Cover the casserole and bake in the centre of a very moderate oven, 325°F., Gas Mark 3, for 1¼ hours. Any liquid left could be served with the meat, or served Moroccan style in a separate bowl, seasoned with a little chilli powder. Serve with boiled noodles tossed in butter and the celery.

To vary: Use sliced oranges and ¼ pint orange juice instead of the prunes and prune juice.

BRAISED CELERY

**1½ oz. fat · 1 large onion · 1 oz. flour ·
½ pint brown stock ·
1 head celery · seasoning**

Heat the fat, fry the chopped onion. Stir in the flour, blend in the stock. Bring to the boil, cook until thickened. Cut the well washed and dried celery into neat portions. Blend with the sauce, season, and transfer to a deep casserole. Cover well and cook in the coolest part of the oven. The amount of sauce in this dish is fairly small as the lamb is cooked with a sauce and you just need enough to keep the celery from becoming dry. Double the amount of fat, flour and liquid if you want a good amount of sauce to serve with meat, poultry or fish.

To vary: Fry 1 or 2 chopped rashers of bacon with the onion, then flavour the sauce with a little red wine and herbs. Root vegetables such as carrots and turnips may be braised too.

TOURNEDOS BEARNAISE

**Sauce: 3 tablespoons white or white wine vinegar ·
3 tablespoons tarragon vinegar ·
1 shallot or small onion · 3 egg yolks · 4 oz. butter ·
½–1 teaspoon each chopped fresh tarragon and
chervil or good pinch dried herbs · seasoning ·
4–6 fillet steaks · butter**

Make the sauce before cooking the meat and keep it hot over a
very low heat. Put the vinegars into a pan with the peeled
shallot or onion. Simmer the vinegars until reduced to 2–2½
tablespoons, then allow to cool. Put the egg yolks and the
strained vinegars into the top of a double saucepan or a basin
over a pan of hot, but not boiling water. Whisk until thick.
While this is thickening allow the butter to soften slightly.
Gradually whisk in the butter – *do this very gradually*. Lastly
add the herbs. Season well. Tie (or ask the butcher to do this)
the fillet steaks into rounds (tournedos). Brush with butter and
follow the instructions for grilling below. Serve with the
Bearnaise Sauce, creamed potatoes and cauliflower.
To Grill Steaks: Preheat the grill to seal the outside of the
meat as quickly as possible. Brush the meat with a generous
amount of butter (or use oil). Grill quickly for approximately
2 minutes on either side. If you like rare meat serve at once,
if not lower the heat and cook for a further 4–6 minutes, or
until cooked to personal taste. Serve as soon as possible.

Banana and Lemon Cream

BANANA AND LEMON CREAM

**1 lemon-flavoured jelly · ¾ pint boiling water ·
4 teaspoons lemon juice · 1 tablespoon sugar ·
½ pint thick cream · 2 egg whites · 5 small bananas ·
20–24 sponge fingers · few glacé cherries**

Dissolve the jelly in the water. Add half the lemon juice and
all the sugar. Chill until beginning to set. To hurry this
process stand over a bowl of ice cubes or use ¼ pint boiling
water in which to dissolve the jelly and add ½ pint crushed ice.
When the jelly is firm whip until frothy, then add nearly ½ pint
thick cream, whipped until it stands in peaks. Fold in the
stiffly whipped egg whites and 3 sliced bananas. Spoon into a
2-pint tin or mould (rinsed in cold water). When set turn out.
Press cream-coated sponge fingers round the edge and top
with the remaining whipped cream, sliced bananas (dipped in
remaining lemon juice) and cherries.

GINGER GRAPEFRUIT

**2 grapefruit · 1 oz. brown sugar ·
pinch ground ginger · 1 oz. preserved ginger ·
½–1 oz. butter**

Halve the grapefruit, remove the segments and mix with half
the sugar, the ground ginger and chopped preserved ginger.
Spoon back into grapefruit skins, spread with butter and the
rest of the sugar. Heat for 2–3 minutes only under the grill.

STEAK AND KIDNEY PUDDING

**Filling: 1 lb. stewing steak · 6 oz. ox kidney ·
(or 3–4 lambs' kidneys) · seasoning · ½ oz. flour ·
water or stock ·
Pastry: 8 oz. flour* · salt ·
4 oz. shredded suet · water ·**
**Self-raising flour or plain flour with 2 level teaspoons baking
powder gives a well risen crust, but plain flour gives a thinner,
more delicate one.*

Cut the meat and kidney into neat pieces; discard any gristle
and skin. Mix with the seasoned flour. Put on one side – do
not add the water or stock yet. Sieve the flour or flour and
baking powder and salt. Add the suet and water to make a soft
rolling dough. Roll out thinly and use three-quarters to line a
2-pint basin. Put in the meat and water or stock to half cover
this. Roll out the remaining pastry to form a lid; damp the
edges and press this on top of the pudding. Cover with greased
greaseproof paper and foil. Steam for 4–5 hours then serve.
Additional gravy may be served or fill up the pudding (after
cutting the first slice) with unthickened brown stock. Makes
4 *large* servings.
To vary: This pudding is excellent if made with lean diced
lamb or mutton instead of beef. Add a light sprinkling of
finely chopped mint to the meat and kidney; lambs' kidneys
can be used instead of ox kidney, but these are more expensive.
Diced chicken plus diced chickens' livers is another excellent
filling.
Sliced onions, mushrooms, and mixed diced root vegetables
may also be used with the meat filling.
Older grouse or pheasant, neatly jointed, may be used in this
type of pudding.

*Ginger Grapefruit, Steak and Kidney Pudding, Brussels
Sprouts*

Slimming Menus

Do not imagine that slimming menus are necessarily monotonous and dull. Obviously, there are many high-calorie or fattening foods you must avoid but if you make slimming meals interesting and imaginative, there is a much greater chance of success. I have planned family menus for 4 people that are relatively low in calories and added hints for the 'non-slimmers' as well.

MENU

HARLEQUIN SOUFFLE OMELETTE WITH BROCCOLI
HOT MELON WITH GINGER

HARLEQUIN SOUFFLE OMELETTE

**6–8 eggs · 8 oz. cottage cheese · seasoning ·
1 tablespoon chopped parsley ·
1–2 tablespoons chopped chives or spring onions ·
2 oz. butter* ·
Topping: slices of red pepper or tomato and green pepper**

*If butter is not allowed on your particular diet you must cook the omelette in a 'non-stick' pan. Heat the pan, without any fat, then add the egg mixture.

Separate the egg whites from the yolks. Beat the yolks with the cottage cheese and seasoning until a smooth well blended mixture. Add the chopped parsley and chopped chives or spring onions. Next fold in the stiffly beaten egg whites. Heat the butter in a very large frying pan. Pour in the egg mixture. Cook steadily for about 5–6 minutes, then put the pan under a medium grill and cook for a further 3–4 minutes until set. Slip out of the pan (do not try to fold) on to a hot dish. Top with slices of red pepper, or tomato and green pepper. Serve at once.

For non-slimmers: Add toast, bread or rolls to the meal and top the broccoli with plenty of butter.

HOT MELON WITH GINGER

**1 ripe melon · 5–6 tablespoons fresh orange juice ·
little ground ginger**

Slice the melon and remove the seeds. Moisten with the orange juice, sprinkle with a little ground ginger and warm in a moderate oven, 350°F., Gas Mark 4 for about 20 minutes or until piping hot.

For non-slimmers: Blend a little preserved ginger syrup with the orange juice and top with pieces of preserved ginger. Omit the ground ginger if wished.

MENU

FISH IN WINE SAUCE WITH BAKED
STUFFED MUSHROOMS
CHEESE AND
STARCH-REDUCED ROLL

FISH IN WINE SAUCE

Fish is a low-calorie, high protein food, so is ideal for slimmers.

**fillets of whiting, plaice, sole or other white fish ·
seasoning · dry white wine ·
few halved de-seeded grapes ·
little diced green and red pepper**

Season and fold the fish fillets. Put into a shallow oven-proof dish. Cover with dry inexpensive white wine, add the grapes and diced peppers and cover the dish. Bake for 20–30 minutes (according to the size of the fillets) in the centre of a moderate oven, 375°F., Gas Mark 4–5.

BAKED STUFFED MUSHROOMS

**8–12 oz. fairly large mushrooms · 2–3 large tomatoes ·
1 small onion · 1 oz. butter or margarine ·
1 tablespoon chopped parsley · seasoning**

Wash the mushrooms and remove the stalks. Chop these and blend with the skinned chopped tomatoes, the grated onion, butter or margarine, parsley and seasoning. Put the mushrooms on a large greased oven-proof dish. Top with the stuffing. Cover with foil and cook in the oven for the same length of time as the fish. Serve hot.

For non-slimmers: Top the mushrooms with a little butter or margarine and serve another cooked vegetable with the meal.

To vary: Add a little finely chopped, lean ham to the stuffing.

Add a little made mustard or Worcestershire sauce to the stuffing.

*Harlequin Soufflé Omelette with Broccoli,
Hot Melon with Ginger*

PRAWNS IN ASPIC

**4–6 oz. shelled prawns · ¾ pint aspic jelly ·
1 tablespoon concentrated tomato purée ·
few drops Worcestershire sauce**

Put the prawns into 4 small moulds or dishes. Make up the aspic jelly according to the instructions on the packet. Add the tomato purée and Worcestershire sauce and pour over the prawns. Leave to set. Turn out of the moulds or leave in the dishes.

For non-slimmers : Top with a spoonful of mayonnaise.

STUFFED STEAKS

**4 fairly thick fillet or rump steaks ·
2 lambs' kidneys · seasoning · little chopped parsley ·
2 skinned, chopped tomatoes · melted fat**

Cut horizontally across three-quarters of each steak to make a 'pocket'. Chop the kidneys finely, season well and add the parsley and tomatoes. Insert the stuffing into the steaks and grill until as cooked as you like. Use the minimum amount of melted fat to baste the meat. If preferred, wrap each steak in a square of foil and bake for 20–35 minutes (depending upon how you like the meat cooked) in a hot oven, 425°F., Gas Mark 7; 20 minutes will give a very 'rare' steak. Serve with freshly cooked or frozen spinach.

For non-slimmers : Blend a little chopped bacon or good knob of butter with the kidney filling. The spinach can be sieved or chopped and blended with a little thick cream. Season well.

To vary : Use 6 oz. lamb's or calf's liver in place of kidney in the stuffing.

Use fillet of veal in place of steak. Lay the veal on a board and divide the filling between the four pieces of meat. Roll up and secure with wooden skewers or fine string. Bake in foil in a hot oven, for about 35–45 minutes.

JUNKETS

**1 pint skimmed milk · little sugar substitute ·
2 teaspoons rennet · grated nutmeg ·
Topping: fresh fruit**

Heat the skimmed milk to blood heat. Add a little sugar substitute. Add the rennet (this amount is necessary with pasteurised milk). Pour into 4 dishes, top with grated nutmeg and allow to clot at room temperature. Top with a few slices of any fresh unsweetened fruit (oranges are particularly good but avoid banana) just before serving.

For non-slimmers : Spoon lightly whipped cream (sweetened to taste) on the junkets then add the fruit. Do not break the junket otherwise it becomes 'watery'.

Stuffed Steaks

Watercress Eggs

MENU

**WATERCRESS EGGS
DEVILLED WHITE FISH
WITH GRILLED TOMATOES
AND SPINACH
YOGHOURT AND ORANGE
SUNDAE**

WATERCRESS EGGS

**4 eggs · seasoning · squeeze lemon juice ·
2 tablespoons skimmed milk ·
3–4 tablespoons chopped watercress leaves · lettuce**

Hard boil the eggs and halve lengthways. Remove the yolks, mash with seasoning. Add the lemon juice, skimmed milk (to give a soft consistency) and the chopped watercress leaves. Press into the white cases and serve on a bed of lettuce.
Note: If you are being extra careful with calories, have half an egg only as an hors d'oeuvre.
For non-slimmers: Top each portion with mayonnaise.
To vary: Use chopped canned asparagus tips in place of watercress.

DEVILLED WHITE FISH

**1–2 teaspoons Worcestershire sauce ·
½ teaspoon curry powder · pinch cayenne pepper ·
¼–½ teaspoon celery salt · 1 oz. butter, melted ·
4 portions white fish**

Blend the Worcestershire sauce, curry powder, cayenne pepper and celery salt with the melted butter. Brush over the fish portions and cook under a hot grill. Serve with grilled tomatoes and cooked spinach.
For non-slimmers: Top the grilled fish with a generous portion of extra flavoured butter.
To vary: Use lemon butter, parsley butter, tomato butter or anchovy butter.
Cooked spinach: Do not cream the spinach or add any butter. Season well and add a little grated nutmeg.

YOGHOURT AND ORANGE SUNDAE

6 oranges · natural yoghourt

Cut the peel from the oranges and then cut the fruit into rings or segments. Divide between 4 glasses and top with natural yoghourt.
For non-slimmers: Add a generous portion of sweetened whipped cream or sweeten the orange slices (honey or brown sugar is delicious).

CLEAR TOMATO SOUP

**1 pint canned tomato juice · 2–3 sticks celery ·
6–8 spring onions · sprig parsley · seasoning ·
$\frac{1}{4}$ pint yoghourt (optional)**

Heat the tomato juice, add the finely chopped celery, spring
onions, parsley and seasoning. The soup can be topped with a
spoonful of yoghourt if wished.

For non-slimmers : Top each portion with a little soured cream or a spoonful of thick fresh cream.

To vary: This is delicious as an ice-cold soup for hot weather.

CITRUS LAMB CUTLETS

lamb cutlets · oranges

Bake or grill lamb cutlets or chops – do not fry these. Add slices of orange to the grill or roasting tin a few minutes before the meat is cooked.

For non-slimmers : Serve with jacket, creamed or new potatoes.

GREEN SALAD

Eat plenty of green salads when on a slimming diet – they are low in calories and give you valuable vitamins and mineral salts. Choose the low-calorie salad ingredients, i.e. lettuce, endive, chicory, cucumber and green or red pepper. Shred or chop and arrange a generous portion of salad in bowls or on plates. To make a low-calorie dressing, blend natural yoghourt with plenty of seasoning and a squeeze of lemon juice.

FROSTED APPLE

1 lb. apples · sugar substitute · 2 eggs

Cook the peeled and cored apples until a smooth thick purée. Add a little sugar substitute to sweeten. Allow to cool. Blend the egg yolks with the apple, then fold in the stiffly beaten egg whites. Freeze lightly.

For non-slimmers : Top each portion with cream or vanilla ice cream, and chopped nuts or grated or desiccated coconut.

Clear Tomato Soup, Citrus Lamb Cutlets with Green Salad

Light Meal Menus

There are a number of occasions when a light menu is required. Many people dislike a heavy luncheon, particularly when working hard. A light meal is ideal for a high tea, a late supper or when one is over-tired or has some digestive disorder. If light meals are chosen for medical reasons, avoid highly spiced or exotic dishes containing rich sauces. There are many interesting dishes based on milk, eggs and fish which are easily digested.

All menus in this chapter serve 4 unless stated otherwise.

MENU

**OMELETTE ESPAGNOLE WITH BROCCOLI
COTTAGE CHEESE AND APPLE RINGS WITH BISCUITS AND BUTTER**

MENU

**WALDORF SALAD
CURRIED SEA-FOOD SCALLOPS
CHEESE AND BISCUITS**

OMELETTE ESPAGNOLE
This has almost exactly the same kind of ingredients as the usual Tortilla (Spanish Omelette) but the omelette is a soufflé type.

**1 onion · 2–3 skinned tomatoes · 1 green pepper ·
few mushrooms · little oil · 2–3 tablespoons stock ·
seasoning · strips cooked ham or sausage (optional) ·
diced cooked potato and any other cooked vegetables,
e.g. peas, carrots, onions · 2 oz. butter · 5–6 eggs ·
2 tablespoons milk**

Chop the onion, tomatoes, green pepper and mushrooms and fry in the oil for a few minutes. Add the stock so the mixture is kept hot and moist. Season well and put in strips of cooked ham or sausage if wished, together with the diced cooked potato and any other vegetables. Put the butter into a large, shallow oven-proof dish; put this into the oven to heat. Beat the egg yolks with seasoning and the milk, then fold in the stiffly whisked egg whites. Remove the dish from the oven and pour in the omelette mixture. Bake for about 15 minutes above the centre of a hot oven 425°F., Gas Mark 7 until lightly set. Slip out of the dish if wished, top with the hot vegetable mixture and serve at once.

To vary: If preferred, cook as ordinary omelettes and fill with the mixture.

COTTAGE CHEESE AND APPLE RINGS

**4 dessert apples · 4 oz. cottage cheese · 2 oz. raisins ·
1–2 oz. nuts**

Core the apples and cut into rings, spread with the cottage cheese and top with raisins and/or nuts. Serve with cheese biscuits and butter.

To vary: Use a light cream cheese.

WALDORF SALAD
This rather sweet salad is a pleasant start to a meal and is very refreshing

**1 crisp lettuce · 2 dessert apples · few sticks celery ·
3 tablespoons mayonnaise ·
1–2 oz. chopped walnuts, cashew nuts or almonds ·
Garnish: few fresh or well drained canned grapefruit
segments · grapes or melon balls**

Put a layer of lettuce into a salad bowl. Core and dice apples, chop the celery. Mix these with the mayonnaise and pile on to the lettuce. Top with chopped walnuts. Garnish with the grapefruit segments and grapes or melon balls.

CURRIED SEA-FOOD SCALLOPS

**1½ oz. butter or margarine · 1½ oz. flour ·
1–2 teaspoons curry powder · ½ pint milk · seasoning ·
2–3 tablespoons thin cream · about 1 lb. mixed fish★ ·
Topping: fine breadcrumbs
Garnish (optional): unshelled prawns**
★i.e. flaked cooked white fish, shell fish, either prawns, scallops, or canned or fresh crab meat and a little canned tuna

Make a creamy curry sauce with the butter or margarine, flour, curry powder and milk. When thickened add seasoning and the thin cream. Blend with the mixed fish. Put into scallop shells. Top with fine breadcrumbs and heat under the grill or in the oven. Garnish with prawns if wished.

To vary: To make a more substantial dish, arrange a layer of cooked long grain rice in a shallow heat-proof dish. Top with the curry mixture and heat as above.

The sauce may be flavoured with cheese, anchovy essence or parsley instead of curry

Waldorf Salad, Curried Sea-Food Scallops, Cheese

Mexican Frankfurters

BOILED HAM

Either serve the cooked ham cold, or heat in a little stock or water with a stock cube. Slice neatly.

SWEET AND SOUR ONIONS

**2 teaspoons cornflour · $\frac{1}{4}$ pint white wine vinegar ·
2 tablespoons honey · 2–3 tablespoons tomato chutney ·
$\frac{1}{4}$ pint white stock · seasoning ·
1 large cooked beetroot · about 12 pickled onions**

Blend the cornflour with the vinegar, honey, tomato chutney, white stock and seasoning. Put into a pan and cook until thickened. Add the beetroot, finely diced or grated, and cool. Pour over the well drained onions and leave for several hours.

MUSHROOM SALAD

**4–6 oz. button mushrooms · seasoning ·
3 tablespoons oil · 1$\frac{1}{2}$ tablespoons vinegar ·
fresh herbs (optional)**

Slice the well washed and dried mushrooms, toss in well seasoned oil and vinegar and top with chopped fresh herbs, if wished.

CUCUMBER YOGHOURT SALAD

**$\frac{1}{2}$ cucumber · 10 oz. ($\frac{1}{2}$ pint) natural yoghourt ·
seasoning · squeeze lemon juice · shake paprika**

Slice the cucumber and mix with, or top with, the yoghourt mixed with seasoning, lemon juice and paprika. Serve very cold.

MEXICAN FRANKFURTERS

**3 oz. shell or other shaped noodles · salt ·
1 medium-sized can or $\frac{1}{2}$ pint home-made consommé ·
few drops chilli sauce · 4 tomatoes · 6–8 Frankfurters ·
Garnish: 2 pineapple rings · 1 tomato · parsley**

Cook the noodles in boiling salted water, drain and mix with the consommé, chilli sauce and sliced tomatoes and Frankfurters. Heat steadily for 20 minutes. Put into the serving dish and top with pineapple rings, sliced tomato and parsley sprigs or chopped parsley.

44

SALAD SANDWICH LOAF

1 small white or brown sandwich loaf ·
3 oz. butter or margarine · 12 oz. cream cheese ·
3–4 skinned tomatoes (see below) · seasoning ·
piece cucumber · 3–4 oz. canned or cooked salmon ·
3–4 hard boiled eggs · 3 tablespoons mayonnaise ·
1 lettuce · 3 oz. salted peanuts ·
Garnish: cucumber · radish roses (see below) ·
anchovy fillets

TOMATO SOUFFLES

4 very large firm tomatoes* · seasoning · 3 egg yolks ·
about 2 tablespoons fine breadcrumbs or smooth
mashed potato ·
1–2 teaspoons finely chopped chives or spring onion ·
2 egg whites
* or use 8 smaller tomatoes.

Halve the tomatoes and scoop out the pulp carefully so the
tomato cases are left intact. Season the cases. Chop the pulp
very finely, add the egg yolks and breadcrumbs or potato to
make a creamy consistency. Blend with a generous amount of
seasoning and the chopped chives or spring onion; fold in the
stiffly beaten egg whites. Spoon the mixture into the tomato
cases. Stand on a flat oven-proof dish and bake for about
12 minutes in a moderately hot oven, 375–400 F., Gas Mark
5–6. Serve at once.
To vary: Use grated cheese in place of breadcrumbs or
potato.
Add a few chopped anchovies to the egg yolks.
Omit the chives or spring onion and use 1 teaspoon chopped
thyme or sage instead.

Remove the crusts from the loaf and cut the loaf into 4 slices
lengthways. Spread each slice with butter or margarine.
Layer 1 Put the first slice of bread on a board and spread with
some of the cream cheese and sliced tomato.
Layer 2 Top with the second slice and well-seasoned sliced
cucumber and flaked salmon.
Layer 3 Put the third slice of bread on this and cover with
chopped hard boiled eggs, blended with mayonnaise and
finely shredded lettuce. Cover with the last slice of bread and
butter (buttered side downwards). Coat the top and sides of
the sandwich with cream cheese and press salted peanuts
against the sides. Lift on to a bed of green salad and garnish
the top with twists of cucumber, radish roses and/or a lattice of
well drained anchovy fillets. The salad can be served separately
if preferred.
To vary: Other fillings can be used in place of those given
above, i.e. scrambled egg and finely chopped green pepper,
cream cheese and chopped nuts or raisins.
To skin tomatoes: Put the tomatoes into boiling water for
1 minute. Lift out, put into cold water, then remove the skin.
To make radish roses: Cut the radishes from the base downwards to about ½ inch. Put into ice-cold water to open out.

Tomato Soufflés, Salad Sandwich Loaf, Fresh Fruit

Crab Bisque

MENU

CRAB BISQUE
AVOCADO PEAR SALAD
This menu serves 4–6.

CRAB BISQUE

**1 medium-sized cooked crab or 1 medium-sized can
crab meat · ¾ pint fish stock★ or water · 1 lemon ·
seasoning · *bouquet garni* · 1 onion · 2 oz. mushrooms ·
2 oz. butter · ½ pint thin cream · 2 egg yolks ·
2 tablespoons sherry**
★made by boiling fish bones or a fish head

Remove all the meat from the crab and put on one side. If
using a fresh crab, put the shell into a pan with the stock or
water, the pared lemon rind, a little lemon juice, seasoning and
the *bouquet garni*. Cover the pan and simmer gently for 30
minutes. Chop the onion, slice the mushrooms and toss in the
hot butter. Add the strained crab stock and the flaked crab
meat and heat gently. Blend the cream with the egg yolks, add
to the crab mixture and simmer. Add sherry.

AVOCADO PEAR SALAD

**3 tablespoons salad oil · 2 tablespoons white vinegar ·
seasoning · 2 large ripe avocado pears · 2 oranges ·
2 firm tomatoes · lettuce · piece cucumber**

Blend the oil, vinegar and seasoning and put into a bowl.
Halve the avocado pears, remove the stones, slice and put into

the oil and vinegar dressing. Cut the peel from the oranges and
cut the oranges into neat segments. Slice the tomatoes.
Arrange the avocado pear, orange and tomato slices on
shredded lettuce, garnish with twists of cucumber. This salad
is delicious for a light main course or to serve with meat or
poultry.
To vary: Serve on a bed of watercress or endive.

MENU

CAULIFLOWER SURPRISE
WITH CRISPBREAD
AND BUTTER
APRICOT DIPLOMAT
This menu serves 4–6

CAULIFLOWER SURPRISE

*This looks like Cauliflower Mornay (cauliflower cheese) but
underneath you have a layer of savoury vegetables that turn this
into a 'meal in a dish'.*

**2–3 medium-sized onions · 2 skinned tomatoes ·
6 mushrooms · 4 oz. margarine ·
1 small can sweet corn · few cooked or canned peas ·
few tablespoons diced ham ·
1 medium-sized cauliflower · seasoning ·
2 oz. flour · ¾ pint milk · 4–6 oz. grated cheese**

Slice the onions, tomatoes and mushrooms and toss in half
the margarine until tender. Add the well drained corn, peas
and diced cooked ham. Heat gently but do not over-cook and

Cauliflower Surprise

keep hot until required. Meanwhile, cook the cauliflower in boiling salted water until just tender. Make a white sauce with the remaining margarine, flour, milk, ¼ pint water from cooking the cauliflower and seasoning. When the sauce has thickened blend about one-quarter with the vegetable mixture and put into a hot deep serving dish or casserole. Put the cauliflower on top. Add the grated cheese to the remaining sauce and spoon over the cauliflower. Brown under the grill and serve at once.

To vary: Grill streaky bacon until crisp, then crumble and sprinkle over the cauliflower.

APRICOT DIPLOMAT

**1 medium-sized can halved apricots ·
2–3 trifle sponge cakes · 3 eggs · 2 oz. sugar ·
¾ pint warm milk**

Strain the syrup from the apricots and reserve 3–4 tablespoons. Put a layer of apricots at the bottom of a 1½-pint greased basin. Crumble the sponge cakes and spread over the apricots. Beat the eggs and sugar, add the warm milk and reserved apricot syrup. Pour over the sponge cakes. Cover the basin with greased foil or greaseproof paper and steam for about 1¼ hours over hot, but not boiling water. By this time the pudding should be nearly set. Lift off the cover and arrange the rest of the apricots over the custard mixture. Cover again and continue steaming for 15–30 minutes. Serve hot or cold but allow the pudding to stand for about 5 minutes before turning out of the basin.

To vary: Crushed pineapple, either fresh or canned, could be used in place of apricots. An unusual and delicious variation is to substitute fresh or canned passion fruit for the apricots.

MENU

SOLE SUPREME
CREAMED SPINACH
RASPBERRY APPLE SUNDAE

SOLE SUPREME

**8 small fillets sole · ⅓ pint white wine · seasoning ·
1 oz. butter · 1 oz. flour · ¼ pint milk · 2 egg yolks ·
2 tablespoons sherry ·
Garnish: small fried croûtons of bread**

Fold the fish, put into a shallow pan, poach in the wine for 6–7 minutes, season well. Meanwhile make a thick sauce with butter, flour and milk. Lift fish on to a hot dish, strain the liquid into the sauce. Stir well. Whisk the egg yolks and sherry together and whisk into the sauce. Simmer for 1–2 minutes only, taste and add extra seasoning if desired. Spoon over the fish and top with the croûtons.

To make croûtons: Dice brown or white bread into ½-inch squares. Fry in hot deep or shallow fat or oil until golden. Drain on absorbent paper.

RASPBERRY APPLE SUNDAE

Blend 2–3 diced dessert apples with a little lemon juice (peel the fruit if wished). Blend with 3–4 cartons of raspberry flavoured yoghourt and add a few seedless raisins and chopped nuts.

BUCK RAREBIT

There are many recipes for Welsh Rarebit, but this is an easy one to make.

**10 oz. Cheddar cheese · 2½ oz. butter · 5 eggs ·
seasoning · 2 tablespoons beer or milk ·
1 teaspoon made mustard · 4 slices bread**

Grate the cheese and blend with half the butter, 1 egg, the seasoning, beer or milk and the mustard. Toast the bread and spread with the rest of the butter and the cheese mixture. Toast under the grill while poaching the remaining 4 eggs. Lift the eggs on to the cheese mixture and serve at once.
Note: If you like a stiffer topping use the egg yolk only and 1 tablespoon beer or milk.

Buck Rarebit

To vary: Put slices of ham on the toast and then top with the cheese and egg.

SOME NEW SALAD IDEAS

As fruit blends well with cheese try some of these colourful looking dishes to serve with a Buck Rarebit or with cheese.
Apple and Celery Salad: Dice the tender sticks from ½ head of celery. Dice several dessert apples and mix with a little mayonnaise, French dressing or lemon juice. There is no need to remove the peel, as this gives colour to the salad. Arrange on a bed of shredded endive or lettuce and garnish with olives.
Pineapple and Orange Salad: Mix diced well drained canned or fresh pineapple with orange segments. Put on to a bed of lettuce, watercress and chicory and top with a little

Haddock Charlotte with Creamed Carrots and Duchesse Potatoes, Peach Madrilenes

well seasoned yoghourt.
Prune and Nut Coleslaw: Mix chopped nuts, shredded cabbage and a few cooked well drained prunes together. Blend with a little mayonnaise.
Pear and Nut Salad: Mix peeled and sliced pears with some chopped nuts and mayonnaise to bind. Put on to a bed of lettuce and garnish with chicory leaves.

HADDOCK CHARLOTTE

**4–5 large slices bread and butter ·
1–1¼ lb. fresh haddock · 1 egg · ¼ pint milk ·
seasoning · 1 teaspoon finely grated lemon rind ·
1–2 teaspoons finely chopped parsley ·
Garnish: segments of tomato and lemon**

Cut the crusts from the bread and butter. Flake the fish finely or put this through a mincer. Blend with the egg, milk, seasoning, lemon rind and parsley. Cut the bread into fingers and put half at the bottom of a 2-pint pie dish with the buttered side touching the bottom of the dish. Spoon the fish mixture over this. Top with fingers of bread and butter with the buttered side uppermost. Bake for 45–55 minutes in the centre of a very moderate to moderate oven, 325–350 F., Gas Mark 3–4, until the bread topping is crisp. Garnish with segments of tomato and lemon.

CREAMED CARROTS

**1 lb. carrots · knob of butter or margarine ·
2–3 tablespoons thin cream or top of the milk**

Cook and mash the carrots, then blend with the butter or margarine and cream or top of the milk. Pile into the serving dish.

DUCHESSE POTATOES

**1½ lb. potatoes · 2 oz. butter or margarine ·
1 or 2 egg yolks**

Cook and mash the potatoes, then sieve to ensure all the lumps are removed. Beat the butter or margarine and the egg yolks into the mashed potato. Do not add milk as this makes the potato shapes spread badly. Pipe or pile into large rose or pyramid shapes on a greased oven-proof dish or baking tray. Heat through and brown in the oven.

PEACH MADRILENES

**12 grapes · 1 orange · ¼ pint thick cream · sugar ·
4 large or 8 smaller peach halves**

Halve and de-seed the grapes, skin if wished. Remove the skin, pith and pips from the orange and cut the fruit into neat pieces. Whip the cream until it just holds its shape. Sweeten to taste. Add the grapes and orange segments and pile into the peach halves.
To vary: Thick smooth custard, soured cream or natural yoghourt may be used in place of cream.

Family Menus

The essence of most family meal planning is to create interesting meals, without being unduly extravagant, or taking too long in preparation.

It is important to give the family meals that are nutritionally well balanced. All the family need adequate amounts of protein. Fortunately there are many ways in which we can obtain protein – from meat and poultry, fish, eggs, cheese, from the pulses (beans, peas, lentils), milk and bread.

These menus concentrate on nutritious meals that provide pleasant tasting and attractive looking dishes which do not require a great deal of time spent on them. All menus in this chapter serve 4 unless stated to the contrary.

MENU

**CHEESE PUDDING
WITH MIXED
VEGETABLES
TREACLE TART**
This menu serves 4–6

CHEESE PUDDING

**4 oz. soft breadcrumbs · ¾ pint milk ·
1 oz. butter or margarine ·
6 oz. Cheddar cheese, grated · 3 eggs ·
seasoning**

Put the breadcrumbs into a basin. Heat the milk with the butter or margarine, pour over the crumbs and leave for 10 minutes. Add the grated cheese, the well-beaten eggs and seasoning. Pour into a 2-pint oven-proof dish and bake in the centre of a moderately hot oven, 400°F., Gas Mark 6, for about 30–35 minutes until well risen and golden brown. Cook diced mixed vegetables until tender, strain and serve with a parsley sauce or topped with tomato purée.

TREACLE TART

**short crust pastry made with 6 oz. flour etc.
(see page 70)
grated rind ½ lemon · 1 tablespoon lemon juice ·
4 good tablespoons golden syrup ·
breadcrumbs or crushed cornflakes**

Roll out the pastry and line an 8–9-inch pie plate. Prick the pastry and bake 'blind' towards the top of a moderately hot oven, 400°F., Gas Mark 6, until set. Meanwhile mix the grated lemon rind with the lemon juice, golden syrup and enough breadcrumbs or cornflakes to give a soft consistency. Cover the pastry with this. Move to a cooler part of the oven, or lower the heat slightly, and continue cooking for a further 15–20 minutes until the pastry is crisp. Serve with cream. *Planning wisely:* The 'tired', rather dry pieces of cheese may be grated, stored in bags or jars in a cool place and used up in dishes, such as the cheese pudding.

MENU

**TIPSY CHOPS
WITH SAVOURY POTATO CAKE
GREEN VEGETABLES
SAUCER PANCAKES AND FRUIT**

TIPSY CHOPS

**seasoning · 4 large or 8 smaller lamb chops ·
4 tablespoons red wine, orange juice or stock**

Season the chops and put into an oven-proof dish. Spoon the wine, orange juice or stock over them; (each gives a different flavour). Cover and cook for 25–30 minutes in the centre of a hot oven, 425°F., Gas Mark 7.

SAVOURY POTATO CAKE

**1 lb. potatoes · 2 large onions · seasoning ·
1 oz. melted margarine or oil**

Peel or scrape the potatoes and slice very thinly. Peel and slice the onions equally thinly. Pack a greased tin with layers of potato and onion. Season well and begin and end with potatoes. Brush the top layer with melted margarine or oil. Cover tightly. Bake in the coolest part of a hot oven, 425°F., Gas Mark 7, for 1–1¼ hours. Turn out like a cake.

SAUCER PANCAKES

**2 oz. butter · 2 oz. caster sugar · 2 eggs ·
4 oz. plain flour · pinch salt · ¼ pint milk ·
Filling: fruit purée (see method)**

Cream the butter and sugar until soft. Beat in the eggs. Fold in the sieved flour and salt, add the milk. Grease 8 shallow oven-proof dishes or tins well and heat, spoon the batter into these. Bake for 10–15 minutes towards the top of a hot oven, 425°F., Gas Mark 7. Serve with hot fruit purée, apple, cherry, raspberry, apricot and gooseberry are ideal.

Cheese Pudding with Mixed Vegetables, Treacle Tart

Stir the grated rind of the lemons into the hot apple purée. Blend the powdered gelatine with the juice from the lemons. Stir into the hot apple purée with the golden syrup. Spoon into a rinsed mould and allow to set. Turn out, decorate with lemon slices and serve with ice cream or cream.

SAUTE POTATOES

**12 oz.–1 lb. cooked potatoes · little fat ·
chopped parsley**

Slice the potatoes neatly. Fry in the hot fat until golden on both sides. Drain on absorbent paper, top with parsley.

APPLE LEMON MOULD

**2 lemons · 1 pint hot *thick* apple purée ·
½ oz. powdered gelatine · 2 tablespoons golden syrup
Decoration: lemon slices**

This menu is designed to turn a very simple one-course family meal into a special one for an increased number of people, i.e. 6–8. The Salad Niçoise is sustaining and interesting, so will help you if you are trying to make meat 'go further'.

Apple Lemon Mould

SALAD NICOISE

1 × 8 oz. can tuna · 1 small can anchovy fillets ·
lettuce · 3 tomatoes · 2 hard boiled eggs ·
8 oz. cooked new potatoes (optional) ·
8 oz. cooked beans (optional) ·
mayonnaise or oil and vinegar · seasoning ·
few black and green olives (optional)

Dice the tuna and separate the anchovy fillets. Make a salad of
lettuce, tomatoes and hard-boiled eggs. Add sliced cooked new
potatoes and cooked beans when available. Add the tuna fish
and the anchovy fillets. Toss in either mayonnaise or well
seasoned oil and vinegar. The salad may be garnished with
black or green olives.

LIVER AND STEAK CASSEROLE

*This is an excellent way of adding liver to a menu. Many people
dislike liver, which is a pity, as it is such a nutritious meat, but
in this casserole the flavour is not too strong. If you add a little
brown sugar and orange juice to the brown stock this 'takes
away' any bitter taste.*

8 oz. lambs' liver · 1 lb. stewing steak · seasoning ·
1 oz. flour · 2 oz. margarine or dripping ·
1 pint brown stock ·
1 tablespoon concentrated tomato purée ·
2 teaspoons Worcestershire sauce · 8 small onions ·
4 oz. button mushrooms · chopped parsley

Cut the liver and stewing steak into small pieces. Coat in
seasoned flour and fry in the margarine or dripping. Gradually
add the stock plus the tomato purée and Worcestershire
sauce. Cover the pan and simmer for about $1\frac{1}{2}$ hours. Add the
peeled onions and the mushrooms, then continue cooking
for a further $\frac{3}{4}$–1 hour until the steak is tender. Top with
chopped parsley. *The casserole serves 4–6 normally, but with the
salad could serve 8 people.*

Planning wisely: Warm the oranges, if using, before you
halve and squeeze out the juice – you will have a bigger yield
of juice. If you have no small onions for the Liver and Steak
Casserole use pickled onions instead, they give a very good
flavour to the dish. When you have time, it is a good idea to
chop several tablespoons of parsley and store it in a covered
container in the refrigerator.

Salad Niçoise

MENU

MIXED HORS D'OEUVRE
APRICOT STUFFED PORK
APPLE SAUCE
ROAST POTATOES
GREEN VEGETABLE
FRUIT PIE
This menu serves 6

A simple mixed hors d'oeuvre turns an ordinary family meal into a special one. It need not be too expensive, and can often incorporate left-over ingredients, such as cooked rice and potatoes, small quantities of salad ingredients and left-over fish and meat. A roast joint is a good choice for a family meal as it is always popular and requires little preparation. If you buy a fairly large joint, as suggested in the recipe below, it will give you plenty to have cold.

MIXED HORS D'OEUVRE

Rice and pepper salad: Mix 2 oz. cooked rice with 1 chopped green pepper and a little onion. Toss in oil and vinegar dressing and top with chopped parsley.
Prawn eggs: Hard-boil 3 eggs, halve, remove the yolks and mash with mayonnaise. Add a few chopped prawns, pile into the white cases and top with whole prawns.
Tomato slices: Toss 3–4 sliced tomatoes in a little oil, vinegar, seasoning and finely chopped onion. Top with chopped parsley.
Sardines: Lightly season canned sardines and sprinkle with lemon juice and chopped parsley.
Onions and cream: Slice 2 onions into rings. Toss in a little thin cream, soured cream or yoghourt and season. Top with paprika or chopped parsley.
Diced cucumber: Toss peeled and diced cucumber in a little oil, vinegar, seasoning and chopped chives.

APRICOT STUFFED PORK

about 4½ lb. loin of pork ·
4 oz. soft breadcrumbs, preferably wholemeal ·
2 oz. melted margarine ·
generous ¼ pint chopped canned or cooked apricots ·
3 oz. raisins ·
1–2 tablespoons flaked almonds (optional) ·
seasoning · 1 tablespoon chopped parsley ·
little apricot syrup · little oil

Have the pork boned so it can be rolled round the stuffing. Blend the crumbs with the melted margarine, apricots, raisins, almonds, seasoning, chopped parsley and apricot syrup. Cooking time includes the weight of the stuffing so allow about 2 hours. Brush the fat with a little oil. Start in a hot oven, 425–450°F., Gas Mark 7–8 and reduce the heat to moderately hot, 400°F., Gas Mark 6, after about 45 minutes. Roast potatoes in hot fat in a separate tin.

APPLE SAUCE

1 lb. apples · little water · sugar

Simmer peeled sliced apples in a little water with sugar to taste. Sieve or emulsify until a smooth purée.

FRUIT PIE

1½–2 lb. fruit★ · water · sugar to taste ·
short crust or flaky pastry made with 6–8 oz. flour, etc. (see pages 70 and 116) · caster or icing sugar
★choose fairly 'sharp' fruit to follow the rather rich flavoured pork, e.g. plums, greengages, mangoes or sharp gooseberries.

Prepare and put the fruit in the pie dish. Add the minimum of water and a little sugar. Top with short crust or flaky pastry. Bake for about 40–45 minutes until the pastry is crisp and brown and the fruit soft. Reduce the heat or lay a piece of paper over the pastry if it is becoming too brown. Sprinkle with caster or icing sugar before serving.
Planning wisely: Make the hors d'oeuvre earlier and put this, on its platter, in the refrigerator or a cool place. Cover very lightly with damped kitchen paper and it will stay fresh looking for 2–3 hours. If you make a quantity of soft crumbs, when you have a little time, store them in jars or polythene boxes in a cool place or in the refrigerator or freezer then you can remove the quantity required for the apricot stuffing or any other stuffings.

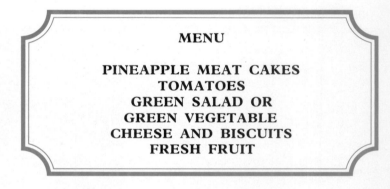

MENU

PINEAPPLE MEAT CAKES
TOMATOES
GREEN SALAD OR
GREEN VEGETABLE
CHEESE AND BISCUITS
FRESH FRUIT

PINEAPPLE MEAT CAKES

1 large onion · 1 clove garlic (optional) ·
2 oz. margarine or fat · 1 lb. sausagemeat · 1 egg ·
seasoning · 4 pineapple rings · 1–2 tomatoes

Peel and chop the onion and garlic finely. Heat the margarine or fat in a pan. Fry the onion and garlic until soft. Blend with the sausagemeat, egg and a little extra seasoning if desired. Form into 8 flat cakes. Fry or grill until the sausagemeat is cooked (about 10–12 minutes). Sandwich 2 cakes together with a ring of pineapple. Top with rings of uncooked tomato. Serve with grilled or fried tomatoes.
Planning wisely: Keep a container of dehydrated (dried) onion in the house and use this as the instructions on the packet when you are short of time – it saves chopping a fresh onion. Use garlic salt instead of crushed garlic.
To vary: Use 1 lb. minced meat instead of sausagemeat; this can be minced beef, lamb or lean pork. If the meat is *raw* prepare and cook as the recipe above, but if the meat is already cooked you will need to add a little thick sauce and crumbs to make it bind together. Fry the onion and garlic in the margarine or fat (as above), blend in ½ oz. flour and cook for 2–3 minutes. Stir in 5 tablespoons stock or milk, bring to the boil slowly, stirring all the time. Add 1 lb. minced cooked meat, 1 oz. breadcrumbs, 1 egg and seasoning. Form into 8 cakes and cook for about 6 minutes only, do not over-cook.

Mixed Hors d'Oeuvre, Apricot Stuffed Pork with Apple Sauce and Roast Potatoes, Fruit Pie

Casserole Menus

The menus that follow are for dishes to be cooked in covered containers in the oven. If you have insufficient casseroles use cake tins, with fixed, not loose, bases or oven-proof dishes. Cover the tins or dishes with foil. If the recipe contains an appreciable amount of liquid it can spoil the cake tin slightly, causing the cake mixture to stick. To avoid this, grease cake tins very well after use as a casserole. All menus in this chapter serve 4 unless stated otherwise.

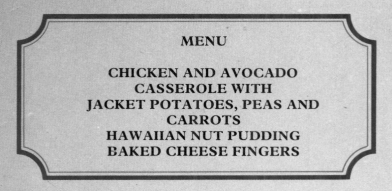

MENU

**CHICKEN AND AVOCADO
CASSEROLE WITH
JACKET POTATOES, PEAS AND
CARROTS
HAWAIIAN NUT PUDDING
BAKED CHEESE FINGERS**

Set the oven at moderate to moderately hot, 375–400°F., Gas Mark 5–6. Allow about 1 hour for the chicken dish with vegetables, 45 minutes for the pudding, and about 15 minutes for the cheese fingers. This menu serves 6.

CHICKEN AND AVOCADO CASSEROLE

**6 joints young chicken · seasoning · 1 oz. flour ·
¼ teaspoon dried, or 1 teaspoon fresh chopped, thyme ·**

**1 lemon · 3 oz. butter · 2 onions ·
½ pint dry white wine ·
¼ pint chicken stock or water and ½ chicken stock cube ·
1 tablespoon flour · ¼ pint thick cream ·
2 ripe avocado pears · little oil**

Coat the joints of chicken in the seasoned flour, mixed with the dried or fresh thyme and the very finely grated lemon rind. Brown in 2 oz. of the butter then put into a casserole. Add the remaining butter to the saucepan. Toss the sliced onions in this for a few minutes, add the white wine and chicken stock or water and stock cube, blended with the flour. Bring to the boil and cook until thickened. Pour over the chicken. Cover and cook for nearly 1 hour in a fairly hot part of the oven. Remove from the oven, cool slightly so the liquid is no longer boiling, stir in the cream. Slice the peeled pears and sprinkle with the lemon juice. Put on top of the chicken and brush with a little oil. Return to the coolest part of oven for 10 minutes. Dice 1 lb. carrots and mix with 8 oz. fresh or frozen peas in a casserole. Cover with cold water, add salt. Cover and cook in a fairly hot part of the oven.

HAWAIIAN NUT PUDDING

**6 oranges · 1 medium-sized can pineapple rings ·
2 oz. butter · 2 oz. caster sugar ·
juice 1 fresh orange or 2 tablespoons Curaçao ·
1–2 oz. chopped nuts**

Cut away the peel from the oranges. Strain the syrup from
the pineapple and measure out ¼ pint. Stand each orange on a
ring of canned pineapple and put into a casserole. Heat the
butter in a pan, add the sugar and stir until the sugar has
dissolved. Add the pineapple syrup and orange juice or
Curaçao. Pour into the casserole and cover. Bake in the coolest
part of the oven. Lift out and cover the oranges with chopped
nuts.

BAKED CHEESE FINGERS

**12 fingers bread and butter ·
sliced Cheddar or Gruyère cheese · 1 egg ·
seasoning · 4 tablespoons milk ·
Garnish: watercress**

Make sandwiches with the fingers of bread and butter and the
sliced cheese. Beat the egg with seasoning and milk. Dip the
sandwiches in this and arrange in a shallow buttered casserole.
Bake in the coolest part of the oven. Garnish with watercress.

*Chicken and Avocado Casserole with Jacket Potatoes, Peas
and Carrots*

MENU

OVEN-BAKED RISOTTO WITH AUBERGINES AND TOMATOES AU GRATIN RHUBARB AND DATE PUDDING

Set the oven at moderate, 350–375°F., Gas Mark 4–5, for 1 hour for the risotto and aubergine dishes and about 1¼ hours for the pudding. This menu serves 4–6.

OVEN-BAKED RISOTTO

**2 tablespoons oil · 1 clove garlic · 2 onions ·
1 green pepper · 4 oz. mushrooms ·
7–8 oz. long grain rice ·
1¼ pints chicken stock or water and 1–2 chicken stock cubes · seasoning · 2–3 oz. sultanas ·
4–6 oz. chickens' livers or calf's liver ·
Topping: chopped parsley · grated cheese**

Heat the oil in a pan, toss the crushed garlic, peeled sliced onions, diced green pepper and sliced mushrooms in this. Next add the rice, chicken stock or water and stock cubes, seasoning, sultanas and diced chickens' livers or calf's liver. Bring the stock to the boil then spoon the mixture into a deep casserole. Wrap foil round the outside of the casserole to be certain the rice does not dry. Cover tightly. Put into the coolest part of the oven. Spoon out of the casserole on to a hot serving dish. Top with chopped parsley and lots of grated cheese.

To vary: Add diced cooked ham or bacon in place of the chicken or calf's liver.
Use other vegetables in place of some of those given above.

AUBERGINES AND TOMATOES AU GRATIN

**2 large aubergines · 1 lb. tomatoes · seasoning ·
2 tablespoons melted butter ·
Topping: breadcrumbs, preferably brown ·
little butter**

Slice very thinly, but do not peel, the aubergines and tomatoes. Put one third of the tomatoes in the casserole, season well. Add half the aubergines, seasoning, 1 tablespoon melted butter, half the remaining tomatoes, the rest of the aubergines, seasoning, butter and the last of the tomatoes. Top with a thick layer of crumbs and a little butter. Put on a lid that does not press down over the crumbs or leave the dish uncovered for a very crisp topping. Bake in the coolest part of the oven.

RHUBARB AND DATE PUDDING

**3 oz. margarine · 6 oz. self-raising flour or
plain flour sieved with 1½ teaspoons baking powder ·
4 oz. caster sugar · 1 egg · milk ·
8 oz. chopped raw rhubarb · 4 oz. stoned chopped dates**

Rub the margarine into the flour or flour and baking powder. Add the sugar, egg and enough milk to make a sticky consistency. Add the rhubarb and dates. Put into a greased 8-inch cake tin or a 2-pint pie dish. Stand this in another container of water; the water should be as high as possible in the container, but not so high that it boils over. Put a sheet of foil over both the pudding and container. Cook in the hottest part of the oven. Serve with fresh cream or custard sauce.

MENU

STUFFED ONION CASSEROLE WITH DUCHESSE POTATOES AND GREEN BEANS COMPOTE OF FRUIT

Set the oven at moderate to moderately hot, 375–400°F., Gas Mark 5–6. Allow about 45 minutes for all the menu, except the potatoes which need 25 minutes.

STUFFED ONION CASSEROLE

**4 large onions · seasoning · 3 oz. soft breadcrumbs ·
8 oz. minced, cooked meat* · 1 oz. margarine ·
¼ teaspoon dried, or 1 teaspoon chopped fresh, sage ·
½ pint brown sauce (see below) ·
small packet frozen green beans**
*pork and ham are particularly good in this dish

Peel the onions and boil in salted water until *nearly* soft. Remove from the water, cool enough to handle. Remove the centre of each onion, chop finely and mix with the breadcrumbs, minced meat, margarine, sage and seasoning. Press firmly into the middle of each onion, put into a casserole. Make a little thick brown sauce (see below) from some of the onion liquid in the pan. Pour round the onions, add the green beans (broken up so they can be spread round the onions) and a little extra seasoning. Cover the casserole and cook in the fairly hot part of the oven.

To vary: Finely chopped raw lambs' kidneys can be used in place of minced meat.

DUCHESSE POTATOES

**1–2 oz. margarine · 1–2 egg yolks ·
1 lb. mashed potatoes**

Beat the margarine and egg yolks into the mashed potato. Pile in shapes on a greased oven-proof dish, heat and brown in the hottest part of the oven.

BROWN SAUCE

**1 oz. fat · 1 oz. flour ·
½ pint brown stock or onion stock
plus 1 teaspoon beef or yeast extract · seasoning**

Heat the fat, stir in the flour and cook for several minutes. Gradually add the stock or stock and beef or yeast extract. Bring to the boil, cook until thickened and season to taste.

COMPOTE OF FRUIT

**1–1½ lb. prepared firm fruit, i.e. apples, plums, pears,
gooseberries or use a mixture of fruit · 2–4 oz. sugar ·
¼–½ pint water**

Put the fruit into a casserole. Make a syrup of the sugar and water and pour over the fruit. Put a lid on the casserole and cook in the coolest part of the oven. Turn or switch off the heat when removing the onions and potatoes from the oven. Serve the compôte with fresh cream or custard sauce. If the fruit is fairly sharp, i.e. gooseberries, it can be sprinkled with a little brown or demerara sugar just before serving.

To vary: Dried fruit, e.g. apricots and apples make excellent compôtes. Soak overnight, then cook as above.

MENU

BRAISED BEEF WHIRLS
MACEDOINE OF VEGETABLES
RICE PUDDING DE LUXE

Set the oven at slow to very moderate, 300–325°F., Gas Mark 2–3. Allow about 2 hours for the whole menu.

BRAISED BEEF WHIRLS

**4 slices beef topside · 3 onions · 6 oz. ox kidney ·
1 tablespoon chopped parsley ·
1 oz. margarine or shredded suet · seasoning ·
6 large carrots · 2 oz. fat · 1 oz. flour ·
½ pint brown stock or water and 1 beef stock cube
Garnish: chopped parsley**

Halve the slices of beef, chop 1 onion and the kidney finely. Mix the onion, kidney, chopped parsley, margarine or suet and seasoning. Divide between the pieces of meat and roll up firmly. Secure with wooden cocktail sticks or string. Peel and slice the remaining onions and the carrots. Put into a casserole.

Heat the fat in a pan. Coat the meat whirls in seasoned flour, toss in the hot fat until golden. Lift on top of the vegetables. Blend the brown stock, or water and stock cube, with the fat in the pan. Pour round the beef whirls. Cover the casserole and cook in the fairly cool part of the oven. Sprinkle with chopped parsley before serving.

MACEDOINE OF VEGETABLES

**4 potatoes · 1 swede · 2 turnips · water · salt ·
little margarine · chopped parsley**

Peel and dice the vegetables. Put into a casserole. Cover with water, add salt and cover the casserole *tightly*. Cook in the coolest part of the oven. Strain, top with margarine and parsley.

RICE PUDDING DE LUXE

**2 oz. round grain (Carolina) rice ·
1–2 tablespoons sugar · 1 pint milk ·
¼ pint thin cream · 2–3 tablespoons sultanas ·
1–2 tablespoons halved glacé cherries**

Put all the ingredients into a pie dish. Cook in the coolest part of the oven until the pudding is creamy and golden brown on top.

Braised Beef Whirls

<table>
<tr><td>

MENU

VEGETABLE RICE SOUP
LAMB LYONNAISE
WITH GREEN SALAD
APPLE CRUMB PUDDING

</td></tr>
</table>

Set the oven at very moderate to moderate, 325–350°F., Gas Mark 3–4. The soup takes about 1 hour, the Lamb Lyonnaise 1¼ hours, the pudding about 1½ hours, but if this is over-cooking reduce the heat when removing the lamb from the oven.

VEGETABLE RICE SOUP

12 oz.–1 lb. mixed vegetables – onions, carrots, tomatoes, turnips
1½ pints hot chicken stock or water and 2 chicken stock cubes · *bouquet garni* **· seasoning ·**
1 tablespoon rice · chopped parsley and/or chives

Choose a really deep casserole so the soup does not boil over. Peel and chop the vegetables fairly finely. Put into the casserole with the hot stock or water and stock cubes, the *bouquet garni*, seasoning and rice. Cover and place in a fairly cool part of the oven. Sprinkle the chopped parsley and/or chives over the soup before serving. Serve with crispy rolls or French bread which can be warmed in the oven for 5 minutes.

LAMB LYONNAISE

1 lb. potatoes · 1 lb. onions · seasoning ·
very little chopped sage or rosemary ·
4 large or 8 smaller thick, *lean* **lamb chops ·**
¼ pint stock or water and ½ stock cube (optional) ·
Garnish: sliced raw tomato and/or watercress

Peel and slice the potatoes and onions very thinly. Put half the potatoes and onions into a shallow, preferably long oven-proof dish. Season very well and top with the sage or rosemary. Put the chops over the potato mixture. Add the rest of the onions then the potatoes and season well. If you like a moist mixture add the stock or water and stock cube. Cover the dish tightly and put the dish in the hottest part of the oven. Before serving, garnish with slices of raw tomato and/or watercress. Serve with green salad.
To vary: Put a little fat over the sliced potatoes and lift the lid 40 minutes before serving to allow the potatoes to brown. Use veal chops instead of lamb.
Add thickly sliced tomatoes to the potatoes and onions.
Add sliced, fried aubergines to the potatoes and onions.

APPLE CRUMB PUDDING

2 oz. butter or margarine · 2–3 oz. brown sugar ·
1 tablespoon golden syrup · 1 teaspoon mixed spice ·
8 oz. breadcrumbs · grated rind and juice 1 lemon ·
2–3 good-sized cooking apples · 2 oz. sugar ·
2–3 oz. seedless raisins

Cream the butter or margarine, brown sugar and syrup. Add the mixed spice, breadcrumbs and lemon rind. Put half this mixture into a greased casserole. Peel and slice the apples, mix with the sugar, lemon juice and raisins. Put over the crumb mixture, then top with the rest of the crumbs and a foil covering or a lid. Bake in a cool part of the oven. Lift the lid when 'dishing-up' the meat course so the crumbs can crisp.

Serve with a syrup sauce.

SYRUP SAUCE

3 tablespoons golden syrup ·
grated rind and juice 1 lemon · ¼ pint water

Mix all the ingredients together. Heat in the oven in a small covered casserole.

<table>
<tr><td>

MENU

PIQUANT FISH CASSEROLE
PAPRIKA SCALLOPED
POTATOES
BROCCOLI SPEARS
BANANA AND COCONUT BAKE

</td></tr>
</table>

Set the oven to moderate, 350–375°F., Gas Mark 4–5. Allow 1¼ hours for the scalloped potatoes, 40 minutes for the fish and 25–30 minutes for the dessert.

PIQUANT FISH CASSEROLE

4–6 oz. mushrooms · 1 oz. margarine or butter ·
1 tablespoon chopped spring onion or chives and/or
1 tablespoon chopped parsley · ¼ pint thin cream ·
2 teaspoons Angostura bitters ·
4 portions or 8 small fillets white fish ·
½ oz. butter · seasoning

Slice the mushrooms, toss in the hot margarine or butter. Add the spring onion or chives and/or the parsley, cream and Angostura bitters. Put the fish into a buttered casserole, season and spoon the mushroom mixture over the fish. Cover the dish and bake in the coolest part of the oven.

PAPRIKA SCALLOPED POTATOES

1 lb. potatoes · ¾ pint milk ·
2 oz. margarine or butter · good pinch salt ·
shake pepper · 1–2 teaspoons paprika

Put the peeled and very thinly sliced potatoes into a 2–3-pint pie dish. Heat the milk with the rest of the ingredients. Pour over the potatoes and cook, uncovered, in a fairly hot part of the oven.
To vary: Omit the paprika and sprinkle the potato layers with chopped herbs, parsley, thyme, rosemary, sage.
Layer the potatoes with sliced onions and season lightly between each layer. Reduce the quantity of milk to ½ pint.

BANANA AND COCONUT BAKE

1 oz. butter · 2 oz. brown sugar ·
juice 2 oranges or ¼ pint canned orange juice ·
4 large or 8 small bananas · 1 oz. desiccated coconut

Heat the butter, sugar and orange juice until the sugar melts. Put the peeled bananas into a casserole. Add the orange liquid and press the coconut over the bananas. Bake in a fairly hot part of the oven.

Above: Vegetable Rice Soup, Lamb Lyonnaise, Apple Crumb Pudding
Below: Piquant Fish Casserole

60

Meals for Children

These menus are planned for families with small children. No busy mother wants to cook two separate meals, one for the adults and another for young children, but the needs and tastes of grown-ups and children are not necessarily exactly the same. It is, however, often possible to adapt the dishes, so they are ideal for all the family; these 'extra' ingredients are given in detail at the end of each dish. Children vary of course; some young children will enjoy adult flavourings so some adaptations may not be necessary. Quantities given are for 2 adults and 2 young children (who would have smaller portions).

MENU

**GRAPE AND MELON COUPE
FRIED LIVER, BACON, AND
BROWN GRAVY
CARROTS AND CREAMED POTATOES
CHEESE AND BISCUITS**

GRAPE AND MELON COUPE

**4 oz. grapes · 1 small, or part of a larger melon ·
¼ pint water · 1–2 oz. sugar or honey ·
½ teaspoon ground ginger**

Halve the grapes and melon. Remove the seeds from both fruits. Dice the melon and arrange the fruit in 4 glasses. Make a syrup by boiling the water and sugar or honey.
For children Cool the syrup slightly and spoon a little over the children's portions (unless they like ginger).
For adults Add the ginger to the remaining syrup and spoon over the adult portions.

FRIED LIVER AND BACON

**4 bacon rashers ·
10–12 oz. sliced lambs' or calf's liver · seasoning ·
flour · little fat if needed · sugar (see method) ·
mustard (see method)**

Fry rashers of bacon for *all* the family *lightly* so they do not over-cook while being kept waiting. Coat the liver with a *very little* seasoned flour and fry in the pan until tender. If the bacon fat is inadequate, add a little extra fat before putting the liver into the pan so it does not dry. Lift out when cooked and make a brown gravy in the pan.
For children Liv is such an important food, that it is worthwhile taking a little trouble to ensure children enjoy it. Liver has a slightly bitter taste, which children may not like, so add a little sugar to the flour coating. When the gravy is made, you can also add a pinch of sugar to part of this. Presentation is important to children, so form part of the creamed potatoes into 2 'nests'. Chop the bacon and liver, pile into the 'nests' and top with gravy.

For adults The gravy can be made more piquant for adults by adding a little made mustard or Worcestershire Sauce.

MENU

**SAUSAGE BOATS
WITH JACKET POTATOES
AND CAULIFLOWER
CRISP TOPPED BANANA RICE**

SAUSAGE BOATS

**6–8 large sausages · 6–8 very thin slices fresh bread ·
1½–2 oz. margarine ·
mustard and/or cottage or cream cheese (see method)
Garnish: watercress and tomatoes**

Cook the sausages. Spread one side of the bread with margarine. Put a sausage in the centre, gather up the sides to form a 'boat' shape and secure with a wooden cocktail stick. Brush the outside of the bread with melted margarine and crisp in a hot oven, 425–450°F., Gas Mark 7–8. Garnish with watercress and tomatoes.
For children Bake really small jacket potatoes, otherwise the meal is too 'solid'. Make the cauliflower look attractive by topping with a little paprika and a chopped hard-boiled egg.
For adults Spread bread with mustard and/or cottage cheese.

CRISP TOPPED BANANA RICE

rice pudding (see below) · bananas · brown sugar

Make a creamy rice pudding, or use canned creamed rice. Put into a fire-proof dish and heat gently. Top with sliced bananas and brown sugar and grill slowly until the sugar bubbles.

RICE PUDDING

Put approximately 2 oz. round grain (Carolina) rice, 1–2 oz. sugar and 1 pint milk into an oven-proof dish. Cook very slowly for several hours.

*Sausage Boats with Jacket Potatoes and Cauliflower,
Crisp Topped Banana Rice*

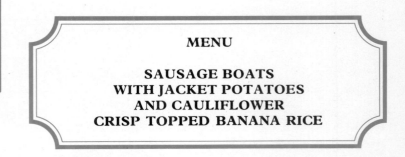

Cheese and Bacon Kebabs, Blackcurrant Flummery

CHEESE AND BACON KEBABS

**4–5 bacon rashers · 8–10 oz. firm Cheddar cheese ·
1–2 ripe eating apples and/or ½ green pepper,
few mushrooms, par-boiled onions (see method)**

Cut the rind from the bacon rashers and cut each rasher in half. Cut the cheese into cubes, then roll the bacon round the cheese. Put the bacon rolls on to a metal skewer.
For children Add segments of ripe eating apple.
For adults Either add apple as above or add rings of green pepper, small mushrooms and tiny onions (brushed with melted fat).
Cook under the grill, turning round until the bacon is evenly cooked. Do not over-cook the cheese as it then becomes less easily digested. Serve on a bed of diced cooked vegetables.

BLACKCURRANT FLUMMERY

**1 lemon jelly · ½ pint very hot water ·
2–3 tablespoons blackcurrant syrup ·
nearly ½ pint evaporated milk ·
Decoration: 4 slices crystallised lemon**

Dissolve the jelly in the very hot water. Cool slightly then add the blackcurrant syrup. Allow to cool and begin to stiffen *very slightly* then spoon into a large basin. Gradually whisk the evaporated milk into the mixture. Pile into 4 glasses and leave to set. Decorate with slices of crystallised lemon.
For adults If the flavour of this dessert is too 'bland', put half the blackcurrant mixture into one basin and the rest into a second basin. Whisk ¼ pint evaporated milk into half the jelly and ¼ pint yoghourt into the remainder.
To vary: Use an orange jelly and the juice of a fresh orange.

BUTTERSCOTCH RAISIN PUDDING

**3 oz. brown sugar · 1 oz. butter · ¾ pint milk ·
3 oz. raisins · 3 oz. breadcrumbs · 2 eggs**

Put the brown sugar and butter into a pan, stir over a low heat until the sugar has dissolved. Cool slightly, then add the milk. Heat gently until the milk absorbs the butterscotch. Pour over the raisins and breadcrumbs. Leave for about 20 minutes to soften the crumbs, then add the well beaten eggs. Pour into a pie dish, stand in a container of water and bake

Salmon Fish Cakes

for about 1 hour in the centre of a slow to very moderate oven, 300–325°F., Gas Mark 2–3.

For children This dessert should be popular with children as well as being nutritious.

For adults The dessert may be too insipid, so serve with lemon flavoured yoghourt, i.e. add grated lemon rind and juice to natural yoghourt.

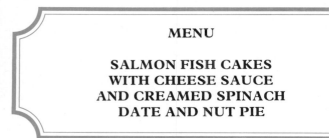

MENU

**SALMON FISH CAKES
WITH CHEESE SAUCE
AND CREAMED SPINACH
DATE AND NUT PIE**

SALMON FISH CAKES

**12 oz. canned salmon · 12 oz. mashed potato · 2 eggs ·
seasoning · ½ oz. flour · 2 oz. crisp breadcrumbs ·
2–3 oz. fat for frying (optional) ·
capers and anchovy essence (see method)**

Flake the salmon and mix with the potato; if using dehydrated potato, make this a little stiffer than usual. Blend with the yolks of the eggs and seasoning. Form into flat cakes, dust with seasoned flour. Brush with the egg whites and coat with the crisp breadcrumbs. Fry in a little hot fat, or bake for about 15 minutes on a well greased and heated baking tray in a moderately hot oven, 400°F., Gas Mark 6 or 25 minutes in a moderate oven, 375°F., Gas Mark 4–5. Serve with a cheese sauce and chopped or sieved cooked spinach, blended with a little top of the milk.

For children or adults Fried food is less easily digested, so bake.

For adults Blend 1–2 teaspoons capers and a little anchovy essence with some of the fish and potato mixture.

To vary: Used flaked canned tuna or cooked white fish instead of salmon.

DATE AND NUT PIE

**3 oz. semolina · 3 oz. plain or self-raising flour ·
4 oz. caster sugar · 3 oz. melted margarine or butter ·
8 oz. dates · 3 tablespoons boiling water ·
2 tablespoons honey ·
1 tablespoon orange or lemon juice ·
2 medium-sized apples · chopped walnuts (see
method)**

Blend the semolina and the flour. Add the sugar and melted margarine or butter. Chop the dates and put into a basin. Add the boiling water, honey, orange or lemon juice and the peeled, grated apples. Stir together until smooth. Sprinkle half the semolina mixture in the bottom of a 7-inch shallow oven-proof dish. Add the date mixture.

Top the date or date and nut mixture with the rest of the semolina mixture. Bake for about 35–40 minutes in the centre of a moderate oven, 375°F., Gas Mark 4–5. Reduce the heat after 20 minutes if the topping is becoming too brown.

For adults Spread a generous quantity of coarsely chopped walnuts over part of the date mixture. These are not very suitable for small children.

MENU

BEEF DARIOLES
WITH HOT COLESLAW
SAVOURY RICE AND
TOMATO SAUCE
ORANGE COFFEE CREAM

BEEF DARIOLES

**2 oz. fat · 1–2 onions · 1 oz. flour ·
¼ pint canned tomato juice or home-made tomato
pulp · 12 oz.–1 lb. freshly minced beef ·
1 oz. soft breadcrumbs · seasoning ·
Tomato sauce: 1 oz. flour ·
¾ pint canned tomato juice or home-made tomato
pulp · 1 oz. margarine · seasoning ·
1–2 teaspoons capers and few drops Tabasco sauce
(see method)**

Heat the fat and fry the finely chopped or grated onions for a few minutes. Stir in the flour and cook for several minutes. Gradually add the tomato juice or tomato pulp. Bring the tomato mixture to the boil and cook until thickened. Stir in the minced beef, breadcrumbs and seasoning. Put into 8 greased dariole tins (castle pudding tins). If these are not available, use old cups or small moulds. Cover with greased greaseproof paper or foil and steam for 30 minutes. Meanwhile make the tomato sauce. Blend the flour with the tomato juice or pulp. Put into a pan with the margarine and seasoning. Bring to the boil and cook until thickened.
For adults Add the capers and Tabasco to the sauce.

HOT COLESLAW

**1 small cabbage · salt · 1 teaspoon caraway seeds
and butter (see method)**

Cook the finely shredded cabbage in the minimum of salted water for a very short time so it retains its crisp texture. Children often enjoy very crisp cabbage and it retains more mineral salts and vitamins.
For adults Try the Continental 'trick' of adding caraway seeds and a knob of butter to the hot cabbage.

SAVOURY RICE

**6 oz. long grain rice · ¾ pint water · ¼–½ teaspoon salt ·
cheese and/or sultanas (see method)**

Put the rice, water and salt into the pan. Bring to the boil, stir briskly, cover the pan, lower the heat and simmer for 15 minutes.
For children A sprinkling of grated cheese and/or a few sultanas will make the rice more interesting.

ORANGE COFFEE CREAM

**2 eggs · 1 oz. sugar · ½ pint warm milk ·
1 can mandarin oranges ·
½ tablespoon sweetened coffee essence ·
½ oz. powdered gelatine (or enough to set 1 pint) ·
Topping: little thick cream · angelica (optional)**

Beat the eggs with the sugar. Add the warm milk. Cook in a basin over *hot* water or the top of a double saucepan until the custard thickens enough to coat the back of a wooden spoon.

Meanwhile blend ¼ pint syrup from the can of oranges with the coffee essence. Put the well drained oranges on one side for the topping. Soften the gelatine in 2 tablespoons cold coffee-orange liquid. Heat the rest of the liquid, add the gelatine and stir until dissolved. Allow both the gelatine mixture and the custard to cool, then whisk together. Put into a mould, rinsed in cold water. Allow to set. Turn out and top with mandarin oranges, cream and a little angelica if liked.
For children The blending of flavours is delicious and should be popular with all the family. Do not give the children any, or too much, cream topping.

MENU

CHICKEN CHARLOTTE
WITH STUFFED TOMATOES
FRESH FRUIT SALAD

CHICKEN CHARLOTTE

**5–6 slices bread ·
2–3 oz. margarine, butter or dripping for frying ·
1 oz. margarine or butter · 1 oz. flour ·
just *over* ½ pint milk, or milk and chicken stock ·
about 12 oz. diced cooked chicken and
4 oz. diced cooked lean ham, or use all chicken ·
chives and/or lemon thyme (see method)
Garnish: parsley**

Cut the slices of bread into fingers. Do not cut away the crusts. Fry the bread fingers in the hot margarine, butter or well clarified dripping until crisp and golden. Drain on absorbent paper. Make a white sauce with the margarine or butter, flour and milk, or milk and chicken stock. Add the diced chicken and ham. Put half the bread fingers into an oven-proof dish, top with the sauce mixture, then the rest of the fried bread fingers. Heat in the oven for a few minutes. Garnish with parsley.
For adults Put part of the chicken and ham mixture at one end of the dish for the children. Add chopped chives and/or chopped lemon thyme to the remaining sauce to make the mixture more piquant.
To vary: Use 1 lb. white fish in place of the chicken.

STUFFED TOMATOES

**4 large or 8 smaller tomatoes · seasoning ·
2–4 oz. cooked peas
and/or 2–4 oz. cooked sweet corn**

Halve the tomatoes, scoop out the pulp, season and mix with the peas and/or sweet corn. Pile into the tomato cases. When tomatoes are at their best serve cold, or heat for a short time only.
For children If the children are very small, sieve the tomato pulp to avoid the pips.

FRESH FRUIT SALAD

Encourage children to enjoy raw fruit. Adapt the fruits in the salad to the children's taste. Do not over-sweeten.
For children Moisten with a little fresh orange juice.
For adults Moisten with a little white wine, or kirsch for special occasions.

Chicken Charlotte with Stuffed Tomatoes, Fresh Fruit Salad

Packed Meals and Picnics

There are many occasions when one needs to take a packed meal. Perhaps you are travelling, and do not wish to break your journey; it may be your husband has no facilities for obtaining a meal at work and has to take packed meals; or maybe it is a family picnic for a day on the beach or in the country. I have added suggestions for Barbecue Meals also where applicable.
All menus in this chapter serve 4 unless stated otherwise.

MENU

TOMATO CREAM SOUP
CHICKEN AND NUT GALANTINE
WITH ROLLS AND BUTTER
FRUIT COLESLAW
CHEESE
This menu serves 5–6

TOMATO CREAM SOUP

1½ oz. butter or margarine ·
small bunch spring onions · 1½ lb. ripe tomatoes ·
seasoning · 1–2 teaspoons brown sugar ·
½ pint chicken stock (see Chicken and Nut Galantine below) · little chopped parsley · cream

Heat the butter or margarine. Chop and fry the spring onions, then add the skinned chopped tomatoes, seasoning, brown sugar, chicken stock and chopped parsley. Simmer for 10 minutes. Sieve or emulsify. Reheat and put into a warmed vacuum flask or chill and put into the cool flask. Take cream separately and use a spoonful to top each portion.

CHICKEN AND NUT GALANTINE

1 medium-sized roasting chicken · the chicken giblets ·
1 pint water · seasoning · 4 oz. chopped nuts ·
2 oz. soft breadcrumbs, preferably brown · 2 eggs

Cut all the meat from the chicken. Put the bones and giblets into a saucepan with the water and seasoning. Cover the pan and simmer for 1 hour. Mince the chicken with the meat from the giblets, when these are cooked, and add the chopped nuts, breadcrumbs, eggs and ¼ pint of the chicken stock. Season well. Put into a well greased 2-lb. loaf tin, cover with greased foil or paper. Stand in a container with a little cold water. Bake for 1¼–1½ hours in the centre of a very moderate to moderate oven, 325–350°F., Gas Mark 3–4.

FRUIT COLESLAW

1 small cabbage heart · 2–3 oz. raisins ·
2 dessert apples · 1–2 oranges · mayonnaise

Shred the cabbage, put into a bowl and add the raisins, the peeled diced apples, peeled diced oranges and enough mayonnaise to moisten. Put into a polythene box, cover, and keep in a cool place.

MENU

ORANGE AND TOMATO JUICE COCKTAILS
CHEF'S SALAD
OLD FASHIONED GINGERBREAD
WITH CREAM CHEESE
This menu serves 5–6

ORANGE AND TOMATO JUICE COCKTAILS

Mix ½ pint orange juice and 1 pint tomato juice. Put into a vacuum flask with crushed ice.

CHEF'S SALAD

6 oz. ham · 6 oz. tongue · 12 oz. chicken ·
6 oz. Gruyère cheese · lettuce · 4 tomatoes ·
3 hard boiled eggs · mayonnaise

Cut the cooked meats and cheese into matchstick pieces, mix well, then put on top of shredded lettuce and sliced tomatoes. Top with quartered eggs. Carry the mayonnaise separately.

OLD FASHIONED GINGERBREAD

8 oz. plain flour · ¾ teaspoon bicarbonate of soda ·
½–1 teaspoon ground cinnamon ·
1½–2 teaspoons ground ginger ·
4 oz. butter or cooking fat · 4 oz. moist brown sugar ·
5 oz. black treacle · 2 eggs · 4 tablespoons milk

Sieve the dry ingredients. Melt the butter or cooking fat with the sugar and treacle, add to the flour. Beat in the eggs and milk. Put into a 7–8 inch square tin lined with greased greaseproof paper. Bake for 1¼ hours in the centre of a slow to very moderate oven, 300–325°F., Gas Mark 2–3. Cool in the tin.

Tomato Cream Soup, Chicken and Nut Galantine, Fruit Coleslaw

MENU

SAUSAGE ROLLS (see page 116)
TOMATOES, LETTUCE
ROLLS, BUTTER, CHEESE
HOME-MADE LEMONADE

HOME-MADE LEMONADE

**6 lemons · 1 pint water · about 4 oz. sugar ·
ice cubes · extra water or soda water ·
Decoration: sliced lemon · mint**

Grate the rind from the lemons. Be careful to take just the top 'zest', i.e. the yellow part of the skin; avoid using the white pith. Squeeze out the juice. Put the water and sugar into a saucepan. Add the lemon rind. Stir over a low heat until the sugar has dissolved, then boil for a few minutes. Cool, add the lemon juice. This is a concentrated lemonade, so it must be diluted.

Crush the ice cubes finely (never put large ice cubes into a vacuum flask, they could crack the lining). Add the strained lemonade. If you wish to dilute this with water pour this into the flasks (use about one-quarter concentrated lemonade and three-quarters water). If you wish to dilute with soda water simply put the concentrated lemonade into the flasks with

Green Pepper and Prawn Cocktails

crushed ice and take bottles of soda water. Top the glasses or jug with lemon slices or mint or put these into the vacuum flasks to give a stronger flavour.

MENU

GREEN PEPPER AND PRAWN COCKTAILS
BACON AND EGG PIE (see page 73)
MIXED SALAD
ICED COFFEE

GREEN PEPPER AND PRAWN COCKTAILS

**4–6 oz. shelled prawns · 3 tablespoons mayonnaise ·
1 large green pepper · 2–3 sticks celery · lettuce**

Mix the prawns, mayonnaise, diced green pepper (discard core and seeds) and the chopped celery. Put into a wide-necked vacuum flask or covered container. Wash the lettuce, shred and carry in a separate container. This salad is highly perishable, so chill until ready to serve.

ICED COFFEE
Put crushed ice into vacuum flasks, cover with cold strong coffee and milk. A little cream can be added or can be taken separately to top the coffee.

Farmhouse Pie

MENU

**FARMHOUSE PIE
HAM AND POTATO SALAD
MIXED SALAD
FRUIT SALAD WITH CREAM**
This menu serves 6

FARMHOUSE PIE

**Savoury short crust pastry: 12 oz. plain flour ·
good pinch salt, celery and garlic salts, mustard
and mixed dried herbs · shake pepper ·
6 oz. margarine or cooking fat · water to bind ·
Filling: 2 onions · 3 large tomatoes · 2 oz. margarine ·
1 lb. cooked or canned lambs' tongues★ · seasoning ·
1–2 tablespoons sweet pickle or chutney ·
beaten egg to glaze**
★or tongue mixed with diced cooked chicken

Make the pastry, sieve the flour with the seasonings and herbs.
Rub the margarine or cooking fat into the flour until the
mixture resembles fine breadcrumbs. Bind with water. Roll
out and use about three-quarters to line a 2-lb. loaf tin. Fry
the peeled and chopped onions and skinned chopped tomatoes
in the margarine. Blend with the diced lambs' tongues (lambs'
tongues are an excellent buy) or tongue and chicken. Season
and add the sweet pickle or chutney. Put into the pastry-lined
tin. Damp the pastry edges with a little water. Roll out the
remainder of the pastry, make a 'lid' to fit on the pie and a few
pastry 'leaves'. Place the lid in position, flute the edges together. Brush the top of the pie with beaten egg, put the

'leaves' in position and brush these with egg. Make 1 or 2 slits
on top for the steam to escape. Bake the pie in the centre of a
hot oven, 425–450°F., Gas Mark 6–7, for about 20 minutes,
then lower the heat to very moderate, 325°F., Gas Mark 3 for
a further 20 minutes. This is good hot or cold.

To make short crust pastry

Use half fat to flour, i.e. 8 oz. plain flour and 4 oz. margarine
or other fat.
Sieve the flour with a pinch of salt. Rub in the fat until the
mixture looks like fine breadcrumbs. Bind with cold water to a
rolling consistency. 8 oz. pastry means pastry made with 8 oz.
flour etc. – *not* 8 oz. completed pastry.

HAM AND POTATO SALAD

**1 or 2 thick slices cooked ham or boiled bacon ·
12 oz.–1 lb. cooked potatoes · chopped parsley ·
little grated onion · up to $\frac{1}{4}$ pint mayonnaise ·
chopped chives**

Dice the ham or boiled bacon, mix with the diced potatoes,
chopped parsley, grated onion and mayonnaise. Put into a
polythene box and top with chopped chives.

To carry salads

Use polythene boxes or bags, foil or a wide-necked vacuum
flask. Wash green salad vegetables, shake dry. Pack at once and
keep cool for as long as possible.

How to make and carry fruit salads

Blend fresh fruits with canned fruit and the syrup from the
can. If using all fresh fruit make a syrup by boiling a little
sugar and water, flavour with orange or lemon juice. Put the
fruit and syrup into polythene containers, with a well-fitting
seal, or into screw-topped jars or wide-necked vacuum flasks.

MENU

**MIXED COLD MEATS
GREEN MAYONNAISE
GREEN SALAD
POTATO SALAD
STUFFED FRENCH LOAF
FRUIT AND CHEESE**
This is one of the easiest picnic meals.

GREEN MAYONNAISE

$\frac{1}{2}$–1 tablespoon chopped parsley ·
$\frac{1}{2}$–1 teaspoon chopped mint ·
$\frac{1}{4}$ teaspoon chopped tarragon ·
$\frac{1}{4}$ teaspoon chopped thyme · $\frac{1}{4}$ pint mayonnaise

Blend the freshly chopped parsley, mint, tarragon and thyme with the mayonnaise. Mix half with the potato salad and carry the rest in a screw-topped bottle.

STUFFED FRENCH LOAF

**For each loaf allow a little butter for spreading the loaf and the filling as below:
2 oz. butter · 1–2 teaspoons made mustard ·
2 tablespoons tomato ketchup ·
1 tablespoon chopped gherkins ·
1–2 tablespoons chopped spring onions or chives about 12 oz. liver sausage or cooked minced or cooked chopped beef**

Cream the 2 oz. butter with all the other ingredients. Split the loaf lengthways, spread with butter and the filling. It is easier to carry the loaf, butter and filling separately and put them together at the last minute.

POTATO SALAD

Mix about 12 oz. diced cooked potatoes with half the green

mayonnaise and 2 tablespoons chopped chives or spring onions or grated onion.

Barbecue tip: If you wish to plan this meal as part of a barbecue, wrap the filled loaves in foil and heat over the barbecue fire. Cook jacket potatoes to serve with the meal.

MENU

CHEESE AND EGG PIE
MIXED SALADS
FRESH FRUIT
MILK SHAKES
This menu serves 6

CHEESE AND EGG PIE

savoury short crust pastry or short crust pastry
made with 12 oz. flour, etc. (see page 71) ·
4 tomatoes · 1 lb. Cheddar cheese · 6 eggs · seasoning

Roll out the pastry and use just over half to line a 9–10-inch pie plate or sandwich tin. Add the sliced tomatoes and diced cheese then break the eggs carefully on top. Season well and cover with the rest of the pastry. Seal the edges and decorate with pastry leaves made from the trimmings. Bake in the centre of a hot oven, 425–450°F., Gas Mark 6–7, for about 20 minutes, then lower the heat to very moderate, 325°F., Gas Mark 3 for a further 20 minutes.

To vary: The pie may be glazed with beaten egg before baking.

Bacon and Egg Pie: Use 1 lb. cooked diced bacon instead of cheese.

MILK SHAKES

Blend flavouring syrups and cold milk. Pour over crushed ice and carry in the vacuum flask.

Mixed Cold Meats, Green Mayonnaise,
Stuffed French Loaf, Potato Salad,
Fruit and Cheese

MENU

**SEAFOOD SALAD
FRIED CHICKEN DRUMSTICKS
WITH TOMATOES AND
FRENCH BREAD
ICE CREAM
FRESH FRUIT**

SEAFOOD SALAD

**3 oz. long grain rice · ½ teaspoon salt ·
6 tablespoons mayonnaise · 2 oz. cooked peas ·
2 oz. cooked sweet corn · 1 small can tuna or salmon ·
3 oz. prawns or canned or cooked crab meat ·
piece cucumber · lettuce**

Boil the rice in salted water until just tender. Drain, toss in the mayonnaise while the rice is still hot. Cool. Blend with the cooked peas and sweet corn, flaked tuna or salmon, chopped prawns or flaked crab meat and diced cucumber. Carry the lettuce separately. As the fish is highly perishable, this salad should be carried in a container in an insulated bag or in a wide-necked vacuum flask.

FRIED CHICKEN DRUMSTICKS

**4 chicken drumsticks · seasoning · 1 oz. flour ·
1 egg · 2 oz. crisp breadcrumbs · fat for frying**

Skin and coat the chicken drumsticks with seasoned flour then beaten egg and crumbs. Fry until the chicken is cooked, crisp and golden brown. Drain on absorbent paper. Any joints of chicken may be fried and taken on a picnic meal, but drumsticks are easier to eat with your fingers.

Barbecue tip: Do not cook the chicken at home, but over the barbecue fire. It is not necessary to coat the joints. Simply brush with oil or melted butter, flavoured with a little made mustard and a few drops Worcestershire or chilli sauce. Cook sausages, tomatoes and jacket potatoes, wrap the French bread in foil and heat over the barbecue fire.

MENU

**CHEDDAR SCOTCH EGGS
LETTUCE AND TOMATOES
SHORTBREAD FLAPJACKS
WITH DESSERT APPLES**

CHEDDAR SCOTCH EGGS

**4 eggs · 3 oz. grated Cheddar cheese · 1 oz. butter ·
seasoning · 12 oz. sausagemeat · 1 oz. flour · 1 egg ·
2 oz. crisp breadcrumbs · deep fat for frying**

Hard boil the eggs, shell and halve. Remove the yolks very carefully, mash, then add the grated cheese, butter and seasoning. Mix well and press back again into the white cases. Put the halves together, then coat each egg in about 3 oz. sausagemeat. Make sure the sausagemeat covers the eggs completely. Roll in seasoned flour, then beaten egg and crisp breadcrumbs. Fry in hot fat until crisp and brown, and the sausagemeat is cooked. Drain on absorbent paper then wrap.

SHORTBREAD FLAPJACKS

**2 oz. butter · 1 oz. caster sugar ·
4 oz. plain flour · milk to bind ·
Topping: 1½ oz. butter or margarine ·
1 oz. brown sugar · 1 tablespoon golden syrup ·
4 oz. rolled oats**

Cream the butter and sugar, add the flour and enough milk to bind. Add as little milk as possible. Press out to an 8-inch round. Put into a greased cake tin with a loose base or on a flat baking tray. To make the flapjack topping, melt the butter or margarine with the brown sugar and syrup in a fairly large pan. Add the rolled oats and blend well. Spoon the flapjack mixture on top of the shortbread. Spread flat with the back of a damp metal spoon or palette knife. Bake in the centre of a very moderate to moderate oven, 325–350°F., Gas Mark 3–4, for about 30 minutes. Mark into sections while warm. Cool in or on the tin. Carry in a polythene box or tin.

Barbecue tip: Warm the Cheddar Scotch Eggs over the barbecue fire and serve with a spicy sauce. To make this, blend 3 tablespoons tomato ketchup, 1 tablespoon Worcestershire sauce, 1 tablespoon vinegar, 2 teaspoons brown sugar and 1 teaspoon made mustard. Spoon over each egg just before serving. Bake apples over the barbecue fire and serve with hot golden syrup flavoured with ginger or lemon juice.

MENU

**COUNTRY BURGERS
WITH LETTUCE
DATE AND NUT FINGERS**

COUNTRY BURGERS

**2–3 rashers bacon · 1 oz. fat · 1 onion ·
4 oz. mushrooms · 12 oz. corned beef ·
3 oz. soft breadcrumbs · seasoning ·
pinch dried mixed herbs or teaspoon chopped
fresh herbs · 2 oz. potato crisps ·
buttered rolls or lettuce**

Remove the rind from the bacon and chop very finely, fry in a pan with the fat until nearly crisp. Add the grated onion and chopped mushrooms. Mix with the flaked corned beef, breadcrumbs, seasoning and herbs. Form the mixture into 8 flat cakes. Roll in the crushed potato crisps then allow to cool. Put in halved soft buttered rolls or between lettuce leaves.

DATE AND NUT FINGERS

**8 oz. sweet biscuits · finely grated rind 1 lemon ·
1 tablespoon lemon juice · 4 oz. chopped nuts ·
4 oz. stoned chopped dates ·
up to ¼ pint sweetened condensed milk ·
1 oz. sieved icing sugar**

Crush the biscuits and put into a mixing bowl. Add the lemon rind, lemon juice, chopped nuts and dates. Mix well, then add up to ¼ pint condensed milk to bind. Coat an 8-inch sandwich tin with icing sugar. Put in the mixture, smooth flat and top with icing sugar. Leave for several hours in the refrigerator to set. Carry in the tin, cut into fingers.

*Seafood Salad, Barbecued Chicken Drumsticks and
Sausages*

Hot Weather Menus

Most of us enjoy hot weather, but it can have a disastrous effect upon one's appetite. If people are very hot and/or very tired, they often lose their taste for food. It is a sensible idea to have a cool, refreshing drink and relax for a while before eating. Do not make the mistake of having all cold dishes in hot weather, this is boring and monotonous; many hot dishes are light and 'easy to eat'. Avoid food that is very solid and take special care that food looks interesting and inviting. Try to cook meals in the oven, rather than on top of the cooker; this keeps the kitchen and the cook cool.

All menus in this chapter serve 4 unless stated otherwise.

MENU

TOMATO JUICE COCKTAIL
SAVOURY CHEESE LOG
WITH GARLIC BREAD AND SALAD
PINEAPPLE SOUFFLE PUDDING
This menu serves 4–6

TOMATO JUICE COCKTAIL

1 pint tomato juice · shake celery salt ·
pinch cayenne pepper · little Worcestershire sauce ·
few bruised mint leaves · 1 egg white ·
very finely chopped mint or parsley

Blend the tomato juice with the celery salt, cayenne pepper, Worcestershire sauce and mint leaves. Chill. Frost 4–6 glasses by brushing the rims with egg white, turning upside down and dipping in very finely chopped mint or parsley. Serve the cocktail in the frosted glasses.

To vary: Add 1 tablespoon chopped chives or parsley to the cocktail.

Add about 3 tablespoons very finely chopped celery in place of the celery salt. Garnish with small celery leaves.

SAVOURY CHEESE LOG

1–1¼ lb. Cheddar cheese ·
2–3 tablespoons each of diced cucumber, sliced
stuffed olives, sliced radishes and chopped walnuts ·
mayonnaise ·
Garnish: olives · halved walnuts · radishes

Grate the cheese finely. Mix with the cucumber, olives, radishes and walnuts. Moisten with enough mayonnaise to make the consistency of very thick whipped cream. Form into a long roll. Garnish with olives, halved walnuts and radishes, chill well. Serve on a bed of green salad with halved tomatoes, cooked peas (topped with chopped spring onions) and sliced cucumber. Serve extra mayonnaise or oil and vinegar dressing separately.

To vary: Other hard cheeses, such as Gruyère, Edam and Jarlsberg could be used in place of Cheddar.

GARLIC BREAD

1 French loaf · 2 oz. butter ·
garlic salt or crushed garlic

Make ½–¾-inch cuts in the French loaf, almost to the base, then pull gently apart with your hands. Blend the butter with the garlic salt or crushed garlic. Spread a little of the garlic butter in each cut. Wrap in foil and leave for about 10–15 minutes in a moderately hot oven, 400°F., Gas Mark 6 or about 25–30 minutes in a very moderate to moderate oven 325°F., Gas Mark 3–4.

To vary: Use 1 tablespoon chopped herbs in place of the garlic i.e. parsley, chives, chervil, rosemary.

Add 1 teaspoon curry powder and 1 tablespoon finely chopped chutney in place of the garlic.

Cream the butter with a few drops of anchovy essence or a few finely chopped anchovies in place of the garlic.

Use 2 tablespoons very finely chopped onion or spring onion in place of the garlic.

PINEAPPLE SOUFFLE PUDDING

2 oz. margarine or butter · 2 oz. caster sugar ·
grated rind and juice 1 lemon · 2 eggs ·
2 oz. self-raising flour or plain flour sieved with
½ level teaspoon baking powder ·
12 tablespoons canned pineapple juice

Cream the margarine or butter with the sugar and grated rind of the lemon. Gradually beat in the 2 egg yolks and flour or flour and baking powder. Add the pineapple juice and juice of the lemon. Fold in the 2 stiffly beaten egg whites. The mixture may look curdled at this stage, but it does not matter. Pour into a pie dish, stand this in a container with a little cold water. Bake in the centre of a very moderate to moderate oven, 325–350°F., Gas Mark 3–4, for about 40 minutes. Serve hot. The pudding separates during cooking; you have a sauce layer at the bottom of the dish with a light soufflé mixture on top.

To vary: Serve with rings of hot pineapple or with vanilla ice cream.

Use orange juice in place of pineapple juice.

Tomato Juice Cocktail, Savoury Cheese Log with Garlic Bread, Pineapple Soufflé Pudding

MENU

MUSHROOM VICHYSOISSE
TERRINE EN CROUTE
WITH NEW POTATOES AND
GREEN BEANS
RASPBERRY PRINCESS
WITH ALMOND SNAPS
This menu serves 4–6

MUSHROOM VICHYSOISSE

**2 large old potatoes · 3 large leeks ·
1 pint chicken stock or water and 1½ chicken stock
cubes · 2 oz. button mushrooms · ¼ pint thin cream ·
seasoning ·
Topping: little cream · chopped chives**

Peel the potatoes and clean the leeks. Chop the vegetables and simmer in the chicken stock for 35–40 minutes. Add the sliced mushrooms towards the end of the cooking time. Sieve or emulsify, cool. Blend with the cream and season well. Top with cream and chopped chives.
To vary: Omit the mushrooms.

TERRINE EN CROUTE

**1 roasting chicken, about 3½ lb. when trussed ·
the chicken giblets · ¾ pint water · 1 onion ·
bouquet garni · seasoning · 2 rashers bacon ·
6–8 oz. lean pork or veal · 8 oz. pork sausagemeat ·
1–2 tablespoons chopped parsley ·
For the pastry: 4 oz. fat, preferably lard ·
¼ pint water · 12 oz. flour, preferably plain ·
pinch salt · 1 egg**

Take all the meat from the chicken. Take care when removing the breast meat, for this must be cut into neat slices. Put the chicken bones, giblets, water, onion and herbs into a pan. Season, cover the pan and simmer for 30 minutes. Remove the lid, allow the liquid to boil rapidly to give 4 *tablespoons* really strong stock. Remove the liver. Put this, the dark meat from the chicken legs and back (leave just the breast meat) and the bacon, pork or veal through a mincer. Season and mix with 2 tablespoons of the stock and the sausagemeat. Slice the chicken breast, put on a dish with the remaining stock and chopped parsley, season. Make the pastry by heating the fat in the water until melted. Add to the sieved flour and salt, knead well. Roll out, use three-quarters of the pastry to line a 2-lb. loaf tin. Fill this with alternate layers of the minced chicken and sliced breast; begin and end with the minced chicken. Roll out the remaining pastry to form a 'lid'. Damp the edges of the pastry, put on the 'lid' and flute the edges. Make a slit in the 'lid' and arrange 'leaves' of pastry on top. Brush with the beaten egg. Bake for 30 minutes in the centre of a moderately hot to hot oven, 400–425°F., Gas Mark 6, lower the heat to very moderate, 325°F., Gas Mark 3, for a further 1 hour. Turn out carefully and cool.

RASPBERRY PRINCESS

Make up a raspberry jelly with ½ pint very hot water. Pour over ¼ pint crushed raspberries, then allow to cool and stiffen *very slightly*. Whisk 3 egg whites stiffly. Gradually whisk 1–2 tablespoons sugar into the egg whites. Fold into the raspberry mixture. Spoon into glasses, decorate with raspberries and chill.

ALMOND SNAPS

**2 large egg whites · 2–3 drops almond essence ·
4 oz. caster sugar · 4 oz. ground almonds**

Grease 2–3 baking trays with oil. Whisk the egg whites stiffly, add the essence. Fold in the sugar and ground almonds. Divide the mixture into 18 balls. Put on the trays; allow space for them to spread out to about 3 inches in diameter. Flatten with your fingers. Bake for approximately 12 minutes just above the centre of a moderate oven, 350–375°F., Gas Mark 4–5. Bake one batch at a time. Remove from the oven, cool for 1 minute. Lift the first biscuit from the tin, roll round the greased handle of a wooden spoon. Remove, put on a wire cooling tray. Repeat this process with other biscuits. Store in an airtight tin when cold. Makes 18.

Fruit Meringue Trifle

Mushroom Vichysoisse

Beat the eggs with the seasoning and water. Make 3–4 large omelettes in the usual way, cooking these in the 3–4 oz. butter. Fill with the lightly cooked vegetables tossed in the 2 oz. butter. Serve at once.

To vary: Use one vegetable only, such as tomatoes instead of a mixture.

FRUIT MERINGUE TRIFLE

**1¼–1½ lb. dessert fruit★ · sugar to taste ·
¾ pint thick cream · up to ¼ pint white wine ·
about 8 medium-sized meringue shells**

★The picture shows raspberries, but sliced fresh peaches, apricots, pears, or a mixture of fruit may be used. Add a little white wine (extra to the ¼ pint in the ingredients) or lemon juice to peaches, apricots or pears to prevent their discolouring. White wine can also be added to the berry fruit.

Prepare the fruit, put into a bowl and sprinkle with sugar. Whip the cream until it holds its shape. Put a little on one side for decoration. Gradually blend up to ¼ pint white wine with the remaining cream. Sweeten to taste. Break the meringue shells (home-made or bought) into fairly large pieces. Put a layer at the bottom of a dish. Add half the fruit, then the cream and wine layer then nearly all the rest of the fruit (save a little for decoration). Top with meringue pieces, piped cream and fruit. This must be served within an hour of preparation so the meringue pieces keep crisp.

MENU

**SALAMI HORS D'OEUVRE
SUMMER OMELETTES
WITH PEAS AND
NEW POTATOES
FRUIT MERINGUE TRIFLE**
This serves 6–8

SALAMI HORS D'OEUVRE

**12 oz. salami · 1 lettuce or other green salad ·
4 tomatoes · ¼ cucumber**

Arrange slices of salami on a bed of lettuce or other green salad. Garnish with sliced tomatoes and cucumber. Serve with mustard or a mustard pickle.

SUMMER OMELETTES

**Omelettes: 12–16 eggs · seasoning ·
6 tablespoons water · 3–4 oz. butter ·
Filling: approximately 1 lb. cooked summer
vegetables · 2 oz. butter**

MENU

GOLDEN TOMATOES
PARCELLED VEAL WITH
YOGHOURT AND SHERRY SAUCE
AND
MIXED SALAD OR SUMMER VEGETABLES
PEACH AND STRAWBERRY
BASKETS

GOLDEN TOMATOES

**4 medium-sized tomatoes · 2 eggs ·
4 oz. cream cheese ·
2–3 tablespoons finely diced cucumber · seasoning ·
thick mayonnaise · sliced cucumber**

Dip the tomatoes into boiling water for about 30 seconds, remove and cool. Take off the skins. Meanwhile hard boil the eggs. Shell, halve and put the yolks on one side. Chop the whites and put into a basin. Add the cream cheese and diced cucumber. Cut a slice from the top of each tomato, scoop out the pulp, chop and add to the egg white mixture. Beat until fairly smooth. Season well. Spoon into the tomatoes, smooth flat on top, coat with thick mayonnaise and the chopped egg yolks. Serve on a bed of sliced cucumber.

PARCELLED VEAL WITH YOGHOURT AND SHERRY SAUCE

**3–4 rashers fairly fat bacon · 4 oz. mushrooms ·
1 tablespoon chopped parsley · 1 small onion ·
2 oz. butter or margarine · 3 oz. soft breadcrumbs ·
1 egg · seasoning · melted butter or oil ·
4 veal chops or fillets of veal ·
Sauce: ½ pint yoghourt · little chopped parsley ·
seasoning · 2 tablespoons sherry · 2 teaspoons capers ·
1 teaspoon made mustard ·
Garnish: lemon · parsley**

Chop the bacon rashers into narrow strips, slice the mushrooms and mix with the bacon. Add the chopped parsley, the grated onion, butter or margarine, breadcrumbs, egg and seasoning. Stir well until the mixture binds. Cut 4 squares of foil, brush with melted butter or oil. Put a veal chop or fillet of veal in the centre of each piece of foil. Spoon the stuffing on top and wrap the foil round the meat and stuffing to make a neat parcel. Lift into a meat tin and bake for approximately 30–35 minutes for thin fillets or 40–45 minutes for chops, towards the top of a hot oven, 425–450°F., Gas Mark 7–8. To make the sauce, put the yoghourt into a basin over hot water, add the parsley, seasoning and sherry. Heat gently, then add the capers and mustard. Unwrap the 'parcels' carefully. Lift on to a dish, garnish with lemon and parsley and serve with the sauce.
To vary: Chicken joints or fillets of fish could be cooked in the same way and would go well with the sauce.

PEACH AND STRAWBERRY BASKETS

**4 peaches or 8 canned peach halves ·
4 oz. strawberries · ¼ pint thick cream ·
1 tablespoon sieved icing sugar ·
Topping: whole strawberries**

Halve the peaches if using fresh fruit. Slice the strawberries; do *not* mash. Blend with the whipped cream and icing sugar. Spread over the peach halves (cut side uppermost). If using fresh peaches make sure the cream mixture covers the cut surface to prevent discoloration. Top with whole strawberries. Decorate with strawberry leaves where possible.
To vary: Raspberries could be used in the same way as strawberries.

SOUR AND SWEET EGGS

**4–6 eggs · 1 large onion · 2 oz. butter ·
1 oz. flour ·
½ pint chicken stock or water and 1 chicken stock cube ·
2 tablespoons brown malt vinegar ·
1 tablespoon honey · seasoning ·
2 tablespoons diced gherkins**

Hard boil the eggs, crack and shell. Do not *over-cook* as they must be simmered for a short time in the sauce. Grate or chop the onion. Toss in the butter for a few minutes. Stir in the flour and cook over a low heat, then gradually add the chicken stock, or water and stock cube. Bring to the boil and cook until thickened. Add the vinegar, honey and seasoning. Put in the eggs and diced gherkins. Cover the pan and simmer for 2–3 minutes.

SALAMI AND POTATO SALAD

**1 lb. cooked new potatoes, diced ·
few cooked green beans · few radishes, sliced ·
piece cucumber, sliced · 2–3 sticks celery, chopped ·
3–4 spring onions, chopped · little mayonnaise ·
lettuce · 12 oz.–1 lb. sliced salami or other sausage**

Mix the potatoes with the beans, radishes, cucumber, celery, spring onions and mayonnaise to bind. Pile in the centre of a bed of lettuce. Arrange the sliced salami or other sausage round the edge of the dish.
To vary: If preferred the lettuce can be served separately as in the picture.

ORANGE CHERRY CREAMS

**4 very large or 6 medium-sized oranges ·
1 orange jelly · ¼ pint thick cream ·
little sugar (optional) · fresh or canned cherries**

Cut a slice from the top of each orange. Remove the pulp very carefully with a spoon. Drain the pulp and put the juice into a measure and the pieces of pulp on one side. Remove any pips and skin from the pulp. Add enough water to the orange juice to give ¾ pint liquid. Heat and dissolve the orange jelly in this. Allow to cool and begin to stiffen then whisk with the lightly whipped cream. Taste and add a little sugar if wished. Put the orange pulp and a few stoned ripe or canned cherries at the bottom of each orange case. Spoon the orange cream over the fruit. Decorate with cherries.

Salami and Potato Salad

Balanced Menus for Beauty

One cannot plan a sensible beauty routine without considering the value of various foods and their effect upon good health and beauty.
The menus that follow are designed to give interesting and appetising meals planned round the many foods that contribute to a nutritious diet.
The footnote after each menu indicates why I have chosen these.
All menus in this chapter serve 4 unless stated otherwise.

MENU

HERRING HORS D'OEUVRE
CHEESE AND ONION HOT-POT
WITH CHICORY COLESLAW
FRESH FRUIT
This menu serves 4–6

HERRING HORS D'OEUVRE

4 medium-sized herrings · seasoning · little oil ·
1 small onion · 1 dessert apple · little sherry ·
mayonnaise · curry powder ·
½–1 tablespoon concentrated tomato purée ·
2–3 tablespoons natural yoghourt · 1 raw carrot ·
1 teaspoon grated raw onion · 1 hard boiled egg ·
lettuce and watercress ·
Garnish: lemon twists

Fillet the herrings. Season, brush with a little oil and grill carefully so the flesh does not break – *do not over-cook*. Cool, then cut into neat pieces. Blend 1 herring with the finely chopped onion, finely chopped apple and a little sherry. Blend the second herring with mayonnaise flavoured with curry powder. Mix the tomato purée with the yoghourt, toss the third herring in this mixture. Mix the last herring with the grated carrot, onion and chopped hard boiled egg. Arrange the four mixtures on a bed of lettuce and watercress. Garnish with lemon twists. For a more savoury hors d'oeuvre use well drained rollmops or Bismarck herrings instead of grilled fresh herrings.

CHEESE AND ONION HOT-POT

1 lb. potatoes · 1 lb. onions · 8 oz. Cheddar cheese ·
seasoning · little melted margarine · ¼ pint milk

Peel and slice the potatoes and onions very thinly. Slice or grate the cheese. Put layers of the potatoes, cheese and onions into a casserole, seasoning each layer and brushing with a little melted margarine. Begin and end with potatoes. Pour the milk over the mixture. Bake in the centre of a very moderate oven, 325–350°F., Gas Mark 3–4, for about 1¼ hours.

CHICORY COLESLAW

1 small cabbage · 1 carrot · 3–4 heads of chicory ·
4 tablespoons natural yoghourt ·
1–2 teaspoons made mustard · squeeze lemon juice ·
chopped parsley

Shred the heart of the cabbage finely, mix with the grated carrot and the chopped base of the heads of chicory (the white vegetable often called endive). Blend the yoghourt with the mustard and lemon juice. Toss the vegetables in this. Put into a shallow dish, top with chopped parsley and arrange the tips of chicory round the dish.

Analysis

Herrings are an excellent source of protein, fat (for creating a feeling of warmth), and Vitamin A which also helps to give a good skin and healthy eyes. Although potatoes are a 'starchy' vegetable, which must be omitted in a very stringent slimming diet, they *do* contain Vitamin C and like all starches (eaten in sensible amounts) provide energy. Cheese gives calcium for strong teeth, bones and nails, as well as protein. This meal has plenty of raw vegetables for roughage.

MENU

GRAPEFRUIT
OMELETTE FILLED WITH
COTTAGE CHEESE AND
CHOPPED CHIVES
SPINACH

Analysis

This is a perfectly satisfying low calorie meal. If you find unsweetened grapefruit too acid, moisten with liquid sugar substitute blended with hot water. Cottage cheese, blended with plenty of chives for additional flavour, makes an excellent filling for an omelette. Cook the omelette lightly, so it is pleasantly moist.

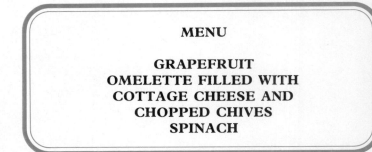

Herring Hors d'Oeuvre, Cheese and Onion Hot-Pot with Chicory Coleslaw.

MENU

AVOCADO SOUFFLE
COLD BEEF WITH
JACKET POTATOES AND
MIXED SALADS
APRICOT FOOL

AVOCADO SOUFFLE

**2 small (or 1 large) ripe avocado pears ·
juice 1 small lemon · 2 teaspoons olive oil ·
seasoning · 3 eggs**

Halve the avocado pears, remove the stones and scoop the pulp from the skins. Mash with the lemon juice, olive oil and seasoning. Add the yolks of the eggs and beat well. Fold in the stiffly whisked egg whites. Put into a buttered or oiled 6-inch soufflé dish and bake for 20–25 minutes in the centre of a moderate oven, 350–375°F., Gas Mark 4–5. Do not over-cook as this soufflé is nicer when not too set.

A delicious variation is to put a layer of shrimps, prawns or crab meat at the bottom of the dish.

Apricot Fool

APRICOT FOOL

**8 oz. dried apricots · ½ pint water · juice 1 lemon ·
sugar or sugar substitute to taste ·
¼ pint thick cream, thick custard or natural yoghourt ·
Topping: flaked browned almonds**

Soak the apricots in the water and lemon juice for 12–24 hours. Simmer until tender. Sieve or emulsify and sweeten with sugar or sugar substitute. Blend with the whipped cream, custard or yoghourt. Spoon into 4 glasses and top with flaked browned almonds.

To vary: The fool can be topped with a spoonful of fresh cream or yoghourt instead of, or as well as the almonds.

*Citrus Fruit Cocktails, Grilled Sole and Cauliflower
Niçoise, Gingerbread with Apple Sauce*

Analysis

Avocado pears are an unusual fruit for they are rich in protein, so the first course of this meal is equally suitable for a light meal. Try to have potatoes cooked in their jackets as often as possible, as you have extra flavour, roughage and Vitamin C. Fresh vegetable salads provide plenty of Vitamin C and are low in calories. Dried apricots are an excellent source of iron.

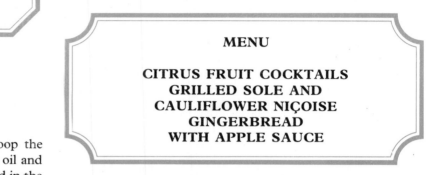

MENU

CITRUS FRUIT COCKTAILS
GRILLED SOLE AND
CAULIFLOWER NIÇOISE
GINGERBREAD
WITH APPLE SAUCE

CITRUS FRUIT COCKTAILS

**1 large grapefruit · juice ½ or 1 small lemon ·
juice 3–4 large oranges ·
sugar, sugar substitute or honey ·
few bruised mint leaves (if available)**

Squeeze the juice from the grapefruit, mix with the lemon and orange juice. Add a little sugar, sugar substitute or honey to sweeten and a few bruised mint leaves when available. Serve in glasses.

Note: If liked the glasses can be frosted. Brush the rims of the glasses with lightly whisked egg white, then turn the glasses upside down over granulated or caster sugar.

GRILLED SOLE

**4 medium-sized sole · little milk · butter ·
Garnish: parsley · lemons**

Soak the fish in a little milk for 30 minutes. Drain, brush with butter and grill. Garnish with parsley and quartered lemons.

CAULIFLOWER NIÇOISE

**1 medium-sized cauliflower · seasoning · 2 onions ·
2 oz. margarine · 4 large tomatoes ·
1 teaspoon cornflour · 1 tablespoon chopped gherkins**

Cook the cauliflower in boiling salted water. Meanwhile chop the onions, and fry in the margarine. Add the skinned chopped tomatoes, cook until a thick purée. Blend ¼ pint cauliflower water with the cornflour, add to the tomato mixture with the gherkins and seasoning. Cook until thickened and spoon over the cauliflower.

GINGERBREAD WITH APPLE SAUCE

Make the gingerbread as page 68. Cut enough portions for 4, warm in the oven and top with apple sauce (see page 54).

Analysis

Fresh citrus fruits are an excellent start to any meal. They ensure an adequate amount of Vitamin C, which is needed daily and cannot be stored in the body. Fish is a low-calorie source of protein, and grilling the most digestible method of cooking. All too often vegetable liquid is not used and this retains valuable mineral salts, so the sauce gives added nutrients as well as interest and flavour to the meal. Black treacle is used rarely, except in gingerbreads, but it is one of the best sources of iron.

MENU

CHICKEN LIVER SCRAMBLE
COTTAGE CHEESE AND
NUT SALAD
YOGHOURT CALIFORNIA

CHICKEN LIVER SCRAMBLE

**4 chickens' livers · 2 oz. butter · seasoning ·
4 eggs · wholemeal toast**

Chop the chickens' livers finely. Heat in the butter, add the well-seasoned eggs and scramble lightly. Serve on or with crisp wholemeal toast.

Yoghourt California

COTTAGE CHEESE AND NUT SALAD

**1 tablespoon chopped parsley and/or mint ·
12 oz. cottage cheese · lettuce and/or other green salad ·
salted or plain peanuts or cashew nuts ·
8 apple rings · mayonnaise ·**

Blend the chopped parsley and/or mint with the cottage cheese. Pile on to a bed of green salad, top with the peanuts or cashew nuts. Arrange the apple rings, dipped in mayonnaise and topped with more nuts, around the cottage cheese. Serve a dish of sliced, well-seasoned tomatoes and cucumber separately.

YOGHOURT CALIFORNIA

**8 oz. prunes · cold water · little grated orange rind ·
little fresh orange juice · natural yoghourt ·
little honey (optional)**

Cover the prunes with cold water, add the orange rind and juice. Leave soaking overnight, then simmer until tender, unless using tenderised prunes which will become quite soft with soaking alone. Chill and serve with natural yoghourt. Add a little honey to the prunes for a sweeter flavour.

Analysis

Wholemeal bread gives valuable Vitamin B and mineral salts. Liver, eggs and prunes are all excellent sources of iron, a mineral that is often neglected in modern diets. The cheese, with nuts, liver and eggs ensures plenty of protein in this meal and cottage cheese, like all cheese, is an excellent source of calcium, while being low in calories. Fresh tomatoes give Vitamin C and yoghourt is one of the easiest and most nutritious desserts. Encourage all the family to eat yoghourt.

MENU

PRAWN AND GRAPEFRUIT
COCKTAILS
ALPINE EGGS WITH
CREAMED SPINACH
MELON

PRAWN AND GRAPEFRUIT COCKTAILS

**2 grapefruit · 3–4 oz. prawns ·
mayonnaise or seasoned yoghourt · lettuce ·
Garnish: tomato slices**

Halve the grapefruit, remove the segments and blend with the prawns. Toss in mayonnaise or seasoned natural yoghourt. Put a layer of finely shredded lettuce into each grapefruit 'shell' or into glasses. Top with the prawn and grapefruit mixture. Garnish with tomato.
To vary: Use sliced avocado pear in place of the grapefruit, and add a few drops of chilli sauce.

ALPINE EGGS

**4 thin slices wholemeal or brown bread ·
1 oz. butter · 4 oz. cottage or cream cheese ·
little finely chopped onion or chives · 4 eggs ·
salt · celery salt · cayenne pepper · white pepper**

Put the bread into a long, shallow, oven-proof dish. Spread with butter, cover with cheese and a sprinkling of onion or chives. Heat for 10 minutes above the centre of a moderately hot oven, 375–400°F., Gas Mark 5–6. Separate the eggs, put the whites into a basin. Pour the egg yolks carefully into the centre of each slice of bread. Whisk the egg whites until very stiff, add seasonings. Pile the meringue mixture round the egg yolks, so the bread and cheese is covered. Return to the oven for 15 minutes, lower the heat to very moderate, 325°F., Gas Mark 3 (this gives time to eat the first course).

Analysis

Shell fish is a low-calorie protein and combines with fresh grapefruit (which gives Vitamin C) for an interesting hors d'oeuvre. Eggs and cheese are as nutritious as meat or fish for a main dish and bread also provides protein. Spinach is rich in iron. Melon has no real vitamin value but is low in calories and very refreshing.

Prawn and Grapefruit Cocktails

Celebration Menus

Something to celebrate often means a special meal. It may be the start of a new job or a new school, a celebration dinner party for an anniversary, or a birthday party. The menus on the next pages give ideas for several different types of celebration meals – from formal dinner or luncheon parties, buffet parties of all kinds to informal wine and cheese parties.

Lobster Soufflé, Veal Chops with Chesnut Purée, Savoury Scalloped Potatoes, Peas French Style, Pear and Chocolate Gâteau

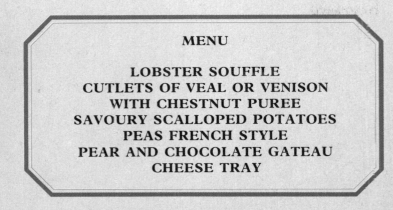

MENU

LOBSTER SOUFFLE
CUTLETS OF VEAL OR VENISON
WITH CHESTNUT PUREE
SAVOURY SCALLOPED POTATOES
PEAS FRENCH STYLE
PEAR AND CHOCOLATE GATEAU
CHEESE TRAY

A special dinner or luncheon menu which would be easy to prepare and serve. Quantities are for 6 people.

Advance preparations: Prepare the fresh lobster stock.

Make the thick sauce in the pan for the soufflé and the thin sauce for the accompaniment, cover both with damp paper. You can emulsify the pouring sauce in a liquidiser before transferring to the double saucepan (see the recipe) to make sure it is very smooth. Prepare the cutlets and chestnut purée. Cut the potatoes, shell the peas; keep both potatoes and peas in cold water. Peel and slice the onions. Make the gâteau, fill and store in a cool place. Arrange the cheese tray.

LOBSTER SOUFFLE

1 small lobster · $\frac{1}{2}$ pint water · seasoning ·
$1\frac{1}{2}$ oz. butter · 1 oz. flour · 3 tablespoons thick cream ·
5 eggs · seasoning ·
Sauce: 1 oz. butter · 1 oz. flour · $\frac{1}{2}$ pint milk ·
few drops anchovy essence ·
about 4 tablespoons thick cream

Brandy Soufflé

Remove the lobster meat from the shell. Put the shell into a saucepan, add the water and seasoning. Cover the pan and simmer for 15 minutes. Measure the stock, put ¼ pint on one side for the soufflé and simmer the rest until it is reduced to 2 tablespoons only for the sauce. Heat the butter in a large pan, stir in the flour and cook for several minutes. Gradually blend in the ¼ pint lobster stock. Bring to the boil, stirring well, and cook until a thick sauce. Draw to one side, then add the thick cream and most of the flaked lobster meat; save the neatest pieces to go into the sauce. Add the yolks of the eggs and seasoning, and lastly fold in the stiffly whisked egg whites. Put into a buttered 7–8-inch soufflé dish and bake for approximately 35 minutes in the centre of a moderate oven, 350–375°F., Gas Mark 4–5 until risen and firm. Serve with the sauce.

To make the sauce, heat the butter in a pan. Stir in the flour and cook for several minutes. Gradually blend in the milk and the small amount of lobster stock. Bring to the boil, stir well and cook until thickened. Add the anchovy essence. Transfer to the top of a double saucepan or basin over hot water, cover with very damp greaseproof paper. Add the cream, any extra seasoning required and the tiny pieces of chopped lobster just before serving.

CUTLETS OF VEAL OR VENISON WITH CHESTNUT PUREE

6 large or 12 medium-sized veal or venison cutlets or chops · butter ·
Marinade: 2 tablespoons olive oil ·
2 tablespoons white wine vinegar or white wine ·
1 clove garlic · seasoning · little chopped parsley ·
Garnish: sliced tomatoes and/or lemon and parsley

Put the cutlets into a marinade made with the oil and vinegar or white wine (you can use red wine vinegar or red wine for venison if wished), the crushed clove of garlic, seasoning and parsley. Turn the cutlets and leave for several hours. This tenderises the meat and counteracts the very dry texture of these particular meats. Lift the cutlets from the marinade, but do not drain. Put into an oven-proof dish, top with a very little butter and cover with foil. Bake for about 40 minutes–1 hour,

depending on the size, towards the top of the oven. Serve with chestnut purée (see below) and garnish with sliced tomatoes and/or lemon and parsley.

To make the chestnut purée, simply heat canned chestnut purée with enough brown stock to make a soft consistency. Season very well and keep hot in an attractive serving dish.

SAVOURY SCALLOPED POTATOES

Follow the recipe variation on page 60 but use 1½ lb. potatoes and 2 sliced onions.

PEAS FRENCH STYLE

1 lettuce · about 1¼ lb. fresh shelled or frozen peas ·
1 oz. butter · seasoning · few spring onions ·
about 2 tablespoons water

Line an attractive casserole with very damp lettuce leaves. Add the peas, butter, seasoning and chopped spring onions. Cover with the water and very damp lettuce leaves. Wrap the *outside* of the dish with foil, so the lettuce does not scorch, and cook on the same shelf as the potatoes for about 1 hour. To serve, just remove the top layer of lettuce. Do not strain the peas; the little liquid in the dish is delicious.

PEAR AND CHOCOLATE GATEAU

8 oz. margarine or butter · 8 oz. caster sugar ·
4 large eggs · 6 oz. self-raising flour or plain flour and
1½ teaspoons baking powder · 1 oz. cocoa ·
2 oz. ground almonds · 1–2 tablespoons warm water ·
1 large can pear halves · ½–¾ pint thick cream ·
little brandy ·
Decoration: browned flaked almonds

Cream the margarine or butter with the sugar until soft and light. Gradually beat in the eggs. Sieve together the flour (or flour and baking powder) and cocoa. Add the ground almonds and fold into the creamed mixture. Add 1 tablespoon warm water to give a soft consistency, or nearly 2 tablespoons if the eggs are only medium-sized. Divide the mixture between two greased and lined 9-inch sandwich tins and bake just above

Sole Normandie

the centre of a moderate oven, 350–375°F., Gas Mark 4–5, for approximately 25–30 minutes, until just firm to the touch. Turn out very carefully. Allow to cool. Drain the pears well. Whip the cream, flavour with a little brandy. Spread some of the cream over one of the cakes, top with sliced pears and the second cake. Spread some of the remaining cream over the cake. Decorate with pear slices, browned flaked almonds and piped cream.

To vary: If wished the sides of the cake can be covered with browned almonds as shown in the picture. First coat the sides in cream and then roll in the almonds to give an even coating.

Suggested Wines
Serve a well chilled Chablis or other dry white wine with the soufflé and a claret with the main course.

```
MENU

PATE WITH TOAST
AND BUTTER
SOLE NORMANDIE
NEW POTATOES
GREEN PEAS
BRANDY SOUFFLE
CHEESE TRAY
```

A luxurious but fairly light dinner menu for 4–6 people.

Advance preparations: Make the pâté at least 24 hours beforehand; it also freezes well for up to 6 weeks. Prepare all the ingredients for the Sole Normandie or prepare the complete recipe and put into an oven-proof serving dish, in which case take particular care that the sole is not over-cooked, and make the sauce a little thinner than usual (add 3 tablespoons extra milk or cream). This allows for evaporation when re-heating the dish. Prepare the sauce for the soufflé, cover with damp paper and prepare the soufflé dish with the biscuits and cherries. Arrange the cheese tray.

CREAMED LIVER PATE

8 oz. calf's liver · 8 oz. pig's liver · 8 oz. bacon · 1–2 cloves garlic · 1 small onion · 4 oz. butter · 1 oz. flour · $\frac{1}{4}$ pint milk · $\frac{1}{2}$ teaspoon finely chopped mixed fresh herbs · 2 tablespoons thick cream · 2 tablespoons brandy · seasoning

Mince the liver, bacon, garlic and onion. Heat 2 oz. of butter in a pan, stir in the flour and cook for several minutes, then add the milk. Stir over a medium heat until a thick sauce. Add the liver mixture and the rest of the ingredients, except the butter, and blend thoroughly. Butter an oven-proof dish and put in the mixture. Cover with well-buttered foil or greaseproof paper. Stand the dish in a bain-marie (container of cold water) and cook for 1$\frac{1}{4}$ hours in the centre of a slow to very moderate oven, 300–325°F., Gas Mark 2–3. Take the pâté out of the oven and put a light weight over the top; this makes it easier to slice. Melt the remaining butter and pour over the top of the cold pâté. Serve with lettuce and wedges of lemon. This would serve 8–10, so there will be some left.

SOLE NORMANDIE
This is a wonderful combination of white and shell fish. Other white fish can be used instead.

1 pint mussels · $\frac{1}{4}$ pint water · *bouquet garni* · seasoning · $\frac{1}{2}$ pint prawns · few oysters · 1 onion or shallot · $\frac{1}{4}$ pint white wine · 8 fillets sole · 3 oz. butter · 2 oz. flour · $\frac{1}{4}$ pint milk · $\frac{1}{4}$ pint thick cream · 4 oz. button mushrooms

Wash the mussels, scrub well, and remove any 'beard' or weed attached to the shell. Discard any that do not close when sharply tapped as this means the mussel is dead and could therefore be 'off'. Put into a pan with the water, herbs and seasoning. Heat until the mussels open. Lift the mussels out of the liquid. Shell the prawns and open the oysters. Add the prawn shells, the liquid from the oyster shells, the chopped onion or shallot and wine to the mussel liquid. Simmer for 15 minutes. Strain carefully and return to the pan. Put the fillets of sole into this; either fold or keep whole if the pan is sufficiently large. Simmer until *just* tender. Lift the sole out of the liquid. Arrange on a flat dish or in individual dishes and keep warm. Meanwhile make a coating sauce with 2 oz. of the butter, the flour, milk and cream and the strained fish liquid. Stir well until smooth. Fry the sliced mushrooms in the remaining butter. Add with the shell fish to the sauce, warm for 1–2 minutes only (so the shell fish does not toughen). Spoon over the fish.

BRANDY SOUFFLE

**about 12 sponge (Savoy) finger biscuits ·
6 tablespoons brandy (or Curaçao) ·
4 oz. chopped glacé cherries · 1 oz. butter ·
1 oz. flour · ¼ pint milk · ¼ pint thin cream ·
2 oz. caster sugar · 3 egg yolks · 4 egg whites**
*or use a mixture of candied fruits

Arrange the sponge finger biscuits in the bottom of a soufflé dish, add 3 tablespoons brandy and the chopped cherries or fruit. Heat the butter in a large pan. Stir in the flour and cook gently for several minutes. Gradually stir in the milk and cream. Bring slowly to the boil, stirring all the time, and cook until thickened. Add the sugar, remainder of the brandy and the egg yolks. Fold in the stiffly beaten egg whites. Pile over the sponge fingers. Bake for approximately 40 minutes in the centre of a moderate oven, 350–375°F., Gas Mark 4–5. Serve at once.

Suggested Wines

A rosé or champagne would be a perfect accompaniment to this menu. Both of these should be served well chilled, preferably in an ice bucket.

```
MENU

LOBSTER THERMIDOR
CHICKEN HAWAIIAN SALAD
WITH NEW POTATOES
HOT MELON AND GINGER
```

This is an ideal hot weather luncheon or dinner menu which is easy to prepare. Quantities serve up to 8 people but the lobster serves 4 as a main dish.

Advance preparations: Make the sauce for the lobster dish, but do not finish cooking until the last minute. Prepare the ingredients for the salad, do not mix until fairly soon before the meal. Prepare the melon and keep this in a covered container so it does not dry. Prepare the sauce and heat at the last minute.

LOBSTER THERMIDOR
This is one of the classic lobster dishes.

**2 medium-sized lobsters · few drops of olive oil ·
2 oz. butter · 1 small onion or shallot · 1 oz. flour ·
½ pint milk · 1 teaspoon chopped chervil ·
½ teaspoon chopped tarragon ·
1 teaspoon chopped parsley · seasoning ·
1–2 teaspoons French or made English mustard ·
6 tablespoons white wine · 3 tablespoons thick cream ·
2–3 tablespoons grated Parmesan cheese ·
Garnish: lemons · parsley**

Split the lobsters, remove the intestinal vein and discard. Take

the flesh from the shells and put on one side. Save the shells and polish these with 2 or 3 drops of olive oil. Remove the flesh from the claws. Heat the butter, fry the finely chopped onion or shallot. Stir in the flour and cook for several minutes, stirring all the time. Gradually blend in the milk, bring to the boil and cook until thickened. Stir well to keep the sauce smooth. Lower the heat, add the herbs and seasoning. This dish *should* have a definite flavour of mustard, but add this gradually to suit your own taste.

Add the wine and cream to the sauce, and *simmer* very gently until a coating consistency again. Add the lobster flesh and heat for a few minutes only. *Do not over-cook.* Spoon into the lobster shells. Top with the cheese and brown under the grill. Serve garnished with lemons and parsley.

To vary: Use large prawns instead of lobster; serve in an attractive oven-proof dish.

Use 2 large crabs in place of the lobster and serve in the well scrubbed crab shells, or in an oven-proof serving dish.

CHICKEN HAWAIIAN SALAD

**4 oz. almonds ·
1 cooked roasting chicken, about 2–2½ lb. trussed ·
1 fresh pineapple · 1 green pepper ·
1 head chicory or few sticks celery ·
¼–½ pint mayonnaise · lettuce ·
Garnish: tomatoes · cucumber or extra chicory**

Blanch the almonds and brown the nuts under the grill or in the oven. Dice the cooked chicken. Cut the top off the pineapple (keep this if the leaves are pleasantly green). Cut the pineapple into rings, cut away the skin and core the slices of pineapple. Do this over a basin so the juice is not wasted. Dice the pineapple. Blend most of the almonds, the chicken, pineapple, diced green pepper (discard the core and seeds) and the chopped chicory or celery. Blend the required amount of mayonnaise with any pineapple juice. Toss the chicken mixture in this. Pile on to a bed of lettuce, sprinkle with the remaining almonds. Garnish with quartered tomatoes and sliced cucumber or chicory leaves. Top the salad with the pineapple leaves if retained.

To vary: Use 2 large oranges in place of the pineapple. Remove all the skin, pith and pips.

HOT MELON AND GINGER
This is an excellent way to serve the less luxurious melons which often have relatively little flavour.

**1 ripe but firm melon · juice of 1 lemon ·
¼ pint water · 2 oz. sugar ·
2–3 tablespoons preserved or crystallised ginger**

Either slice or halve the melon and remove the seeds, then dice the flesh or cut into balls (with vegetable scoop). Heat the lemon juice, water and sugar and the diced ginger. Add the melon and heat for a few minutes only. Spoon into glasses. Serve with cream or ice cream.

To vary: Use 2 tablespoons ginger syrup from preserved ginger and heat with the lemon juice.

Suggested Wines

Choose a white wine for the first course – a Pouilly Fuissé or Pouilly Fumé would be ideal. You can continue to serve this with the chicken salad, but a rosé or sparkling Burgundy would be very pleasant. All these should be served well chilled.

Chicken Hawaiian Salad

MENU

CHICKEN A LA KIEV
WITH GREEN SALAD
AND CREAMED OR NEW
POTATOES
ICED CHRISTMAS PUDDING
CHEESE TRAY

This is a good choice for a luncheon menu or for an after-theatre supper. It serves 4 people. It is better not to have an hors d'oeuvre if you are responsible for the cooking, so you can give your undivided attention to the chicken dish.

Advance preparations: Prepare the chicken dish completely ready for frying. Make the salad. The ice cream can be made and frozen several days beforehand or even longer if wished. Arrange the cheese tray.

Iced Christmas Pudding

CHICKEN A LA KIEV

This classic chicken dish is deliciously simple, except the chicken must be cooked in deep fat or oil until crisp. This is troublesome if you are entertaining. I have experimented by frying the chicken for about 5 minutes until very crisp on the outside, draining this, then putting it on a baking tray to cook for 25–30 minutes in a hot oven. If you wish a slight variation on the usual recipe, blend the butter filling with a little finely chopped red and green pepper, chives and chopped rosemary or thyme. Finely chopped mushrooms can also be added to the butter with a good squeeze of lemon juice.

**4 small young spring chickens or poussins ·
4 oz. butter ·
Coating: 2 eggs · 3 oz. crisp breadcrumbs ·
To fry: olive oil or well clarified fat**

Bone the chicken (or ask the butcher to do this for you). In order to bone the chicken easily do check you have a very well sharpened and flexible knife, for this is essential if you are not to break the delicate flesh. Work slowly so you 'ease' the flesh away from the bones; you should finish with all the chicken flesh intact and free from bones.

Put the bird with the neck towards you. Loosen the skin away from the flesh at the neck end of the bird and gradually work your finger (better than a knife) under the skin over the breasts – do not tear the skin, simply loosen it away from the flesh. Cut away the wishbone with the knife. Turn the bird so the breast is on the chopping board. Cut the shoulder bones from the flesh of the bird and sever these from the body. Cut off the wing tips, discard these; then ease the flesh from the wing bones. Ease the skin away from the flesh of the thighs, then gradually cut the flesh from the thigh bones and the drumsticks. Some people leave the very end piece of the drumsticks (where it joins the foot) as this gives a more interesting shape to the bird, but this is not necessary with this recipe. Work slowly and carefully and cut away the breast bone, back bone and the parson's nose.

Spread the chickens out flat. Put a quarter of the butter on each chicken, roll firmly. Coat with beaten egg and crumbs. Fry in hot oil or fat for 12–15 minutes until golden brown and tender. Drain on absorbent paper, serve at once. Pierce each chicken *gently* before eating so the butter does not spurt out too violently.

To vary: Instead of using a small spring chicken, use the breast of an ordinary chicken. Bone out the breast, then fill with the butter and continue as above.

ICED CHRISTMAS PUDDING

This ice cream can be served throughout the year, but the mixture of fruits makes it ideal at Christmas time. Freeze the ice cream as quickly as possible either in a home freezer, or in the ice-making compartment of a refrigerator. The refrigerator should be turned to the coldest setting 1 hour before the ice cream is made.

$\frac{1}{4}$ **pint milk · 4 oz. marshmallows · 1 teaspoon cocoa ·
1 teaspoon instant coffee · 2 oz. raisins ·
1 oz. sultanas · 1 oz. currants ·
2 tablespoons sherry · 2 oz. Maraschino cherries ·
2 oz. chopped nuts · $\frac{1}{2}$ pint thick cream ·
1 oz. sieved icing sugar (optional) ·
Decoration (optional): Maraschino cherries**

Put the milk, marshmallows, cocoa and coffee into a saucepan. Heat gently until the marshmallows are nearly melted. Allow to cool. Meanwhile mix the dried fruit with the sherry. Allow to stand for 30 minutes then add to the marshmallow mixture with the diced cherries and nuts. Freeze for a short time until slightly thickened. Fold the whipped cream into this mixture and pack into a chilled basin. Freeze until firm. Turn out, decorate with cherries if liked, and serve with more whipped cream (flavoured with brandy and sweetened with icing sugar) or with brandy butter. You can also serve crisp biscuits with the ice cream, if wished. The Almond Snaps on page 78 would be particularly good.

To vary: Use 2 tablespoons brandy or kirsch in place of the sherry.

Suggested Wines

If serving this dish for luncheon a hock would be an ideal accompaniment.

If serving for an after-theatre supper you may prefer champagne or a sparkling Burgundy.

Ingredients for Chicken Kiev (opposite page)

Carpet Bag Steaks

This is a celebration menu for people who like 'good plain food', with a new twist. It is a very satisfying meal – ideal for hungry men and serves 6 people.

Advance Preparations: Make the pudding. Fill the steaks. Arrange the smoked salmon on individual plates, and cover, scramble the eggs at the last minute and put beside the smoked salmon.

CARPET BAG STEAKS

6 *thick* **pieces of fillet or rump steak ·
about 24 prepared mussels or 6–12 oysters ·
4 oz. butter · 3 teaspoons chopped parsley ·
lemon juice · seasoning ·
Garnish: cooked tomatoes · mushrooms · parsley**

Split the steaks to make 'pockets'. Mix the mussels or sliced oysters with 2 oz. melted butter, the chopped parsley, a squeeze of lemon juice and seasoning. Put into the steak 'pockets'. Skewer firmly or sew with fine string or cotton. Brush the steaks with melted butter and grill to personal taste until tender. Remove the skewers, string or cotton and serve garnished with tomatoes, mushrooms and parsley.

BRIGADE PUDDING

**Suet crust pastry: 8 oz. self-raising flour or plain flour with 2 teaspoons baking powder ·
pinch of salt · 4 oz. chopped or shredded suet or butter or margarine · water to mix ·
Filling: 2 tablespoons golden syrup ·**

Brigade Pudding

8 oz. mincemeat · 3 large cooking apples

Sieve the flour or flour and baking powder and salt together. Add the suet, or rub in the butter or margarine and bind with water to a rolling consistency. Roll out very thinly. Cut into 4 rounds – one the size of the base of a 2–3-pint basin, one a little bigger, then the next size and finally one almost as large as the top of the basin. Put the golden syrup into the greased basin, add the first round of pastry, then one-third of the mincemeat, blended with the peeled grated apples, the next round of pastry, then mincemeat and apple, then the third round, then mincemeat and apple. Top with the final round of pastry. Cover the basin with greased paper and foil. Steam over boiling water for 2½ hours. Turn out and serve with cream or custard sauce.

Suggested Wines

A well chilled white wine can be served with the smoked salmon and a claret (Margaux, St. Emilion) or a red Burgundy (Beaune, Beaujolais) with the steak. This is a menu, however, where a beer or lager would be equally appropriate.

MENU

**SALMON WALEWSKA
WITH MIXED SALAD
ALMOND MERINGUE DESSERT
FROSTED CAMEMBERT CHEESE
AND CHEESE STRAWS (see page 118)**

This menu can be served for a formal meal or as a buffet meal. It serves 8 people.

Advance Preparations: Prepare the fish and sauce and cook at the last minute. Make the dessert and put the Camembert cheese into the freezing compartment of the refrigerator or freezer for 30 minutes. The cheese straws can be made some days beforehand and stored in an airtight tin. They can also be deep-frozen, but are best if they are then warmed through before serving.

SALMON WALEWSKA

Although salmon is the ideal fish for this dish it is almost as delicious with cutlets or fillets of white fish, such as halibut, turbot or tuna. Lobster is the shell fish which is traditionally added to the sauce, but others such as crab, prawns and shrimps could be used for economy.

**8 cutlets salmon · 8 oz. butter ·
3 tablespoons lemon juice · seasoning · 6 egg yolks ·
2 small or 1 large lobster ·
Garnish: lemon · cucumber · lobster claws**

Brush the salmon with 2 oz. of melted butter. Sprinkle with ½ tablespoon lemon juice and season lightly. Put into an oven-proof dish, cover with foil, and bake for 20–25 minutes in the centre of a moderate oven, 350–375°F., Gas Mark 4–5, until just tender – do *not* over-cook.

Put the egg yolks, a little seasoning and remaining lemon juice into a basin over a pan of hot, but not boiling, water and whisk until thick. Gradually whisk in the butter then add the diced pieces of lobster. Keep warm but do not over-heat otherwise the sauce will curdle. Lift the salmon into the middle, top with the sauce and garnish with the lemon and cucumber and the lobster claws.

ALMOND MERINGUE DESSERT

**Meringue: 6 egg whites · 12 oz. caster sugar ·
2 oz. flaked blanched almonds ·
Filling: 1 lb. fresh chestnuts plus few drops vanilla essence, or use 1 can (approximately 16¾ oz.)
unsweetened chestnut purée · 2 oz. butter ·
2 oz. sieved icing sugar (optional) ·
¼ pint thick cream · nearly ¼ pint thin cream ·
½ oz. flaked blanched almonds**

Cut out three rounds, approximately 7–8 inches in diameter, of greaseproof paper. Oil each round *very lightly* and put on to flat baking trays. Whisk the egg whites until *very* stiff then gradually whisk in half the sugar. Fold in nearly all the remainder of the sugar. Pipe or spread the meringue over the oiled greaseproof paper to give neat rounds. Sprinkle with the flaked almonds and remaining sugar. Dry out the meringues for 2½–3 hours in a very slow oven, 225–250°F., Gas Mark 0–½. Lift the meringue rounds off the trays while still warm. Carefully peel away the paper, then transfer to wire cooling trays. When cold store in an airtight tin, separating the rounds with greaseproof paper. The cooked meringue rounds can be stored in an airtight tin for several weeks.

To make the filling, slit the skins of the well washed chestnuts and either simmer in water for nearly 10 minutes or roast in a hot oven for nearly 15 minutes. Remove both outer shells and brown skin while warm. Put the nuts into a pan with a little water and vanilla essence and simmer until tender, then sieve. Blend the fresh or canned chestnut purée into the creamed butter and sugar, if using.

Whip the thick cream until it begins to hold its shape, then gradually whisk in the thin cream and beat until firm enough to pipe. Spread the first round of meringue with half the chestnut purée, put on the second round and top with whipped cream. Add the third round of meringue, and top this with the rest of the chestnut purée. Decorate with a piped border of cream and the almonds. Serve soon after preparing so the meringue does not soften. Gives 8 large slices, but will serve 12.

Suggested Wines
A well chilled rosé is ideal for this menu.

MENU

**MELON
VEAL MORNAY
NEW POTATOES
ASPARAGUS OR GREEN PEAS
CHESTNUT AND RUM SWISS GATEAU**
(see page 112)
CARAMELLED GRAPES

A menu that is equally good for a lunch or dinner to serve 4.

Advance Preparations: Slice the melon, keep in a cool place. Fry the veal, make the sauce; reheat this very carefully to prevent over-cooking. Prepare the gâteau and grapes.

VEAL MORNAY

Fried fillets of tender veal produce a delicious dish in a very short time.

**4 thin slices (fillets) of veal ·
4 small slices cooked ham · seasoning · little flour ·
1 egg · 2–3 tablespoons crisp breadcrumbs ·
2 oz. butter · 1 tablespoon olive oil ·
Sauce: 1 oz. butter · 1 oz. flour · ¼ pint milk ·
¼ pint white wine (or use ½ pint milk and omit wine) ·
1 teaspoon French mustard ·
2 tablespoons thick cream ·
4 oz. grated Cheddar or Gruyère cheese ·
Garnish: cooked small new potatoes ·
chopped parsley · lemon ·
cooked peas or asparagus tips**

Flatten the veal with a rolling pin. Place the slices of ham so they cover half of each fillet then fold the meat to cover the ham. Dip in seasoned flour then in beaten egg and crumbs. Heat the butter and oil in a large pan and fry the veal quickly on either side until crisp and golden brown. Lower the heat and continue cooking until tender. Lift out of the pan, drain on absorbent paper. This is necessary as the veal is served with a rather rich cheese sauce. Heat the butter, stir in the flour and cook for several minutes. Gradually blend in the milk and stir until thickened, lower the heat and add the wine, mustard and seasoning. Stir the cream and cheese into the sauce just before serving. Do not allow the sauce to boil. Arrange the veal on a dish in a border of cooked small new potatoes, tossed with parsley. Put a spoonful of sauce in the centre of each fillet, top with a twist of lemon and a few peas or asparagus tips. Serve the rest of the sauce separately.

CARAMELLED GRAPES

**6 oz. caster or granulated sugar ·
6 tablespoons water · small bunches grapes**

Put the caster or granulated sugar into a saucepan with the water. Stir until the sugar has dissolved then boil steadily until a pale golden caramel. Dip small bunches of grapes into the caramel and allow to harden. Eat within a day.

Suggested Wines
Choose a dry white wine, Chablis is particularly suitable, for this menu.

Above: Veal Mornay Below: Salmon Walewska

4 tomatoes into rings. Toss in dressing.

Corn Potato Salad: Blend 2–3 tablespoons mayonnaise with a little oil and vinegar. Blend 3–4 tablespoons cooked or canned sweet corn, 2–3 tablespoons cooked or canned peas and 5–6 tablespoons diced cooked or canned potatoes. Toss in the dressing.

Stuffed Egg Mayonnaise: Hard boil 3–4 eggs, halve and remove the yolks. Mash these and blend with 4–5 chopped anchovy fillets. Press into the white cases. Put into the dish, top with mayonnaise flavoured with a little tomato ketchup and thin cream. Garnish with chopped parsley.

PAELLA

$\frac{1}{4}$ **teaspoon saffron powder or few strands saffron ·
1$\frac{1}{2}$ pints chicken stock · 3–4 tablespoons olive oil ·
2 onions · 1–2 cloves garlic ·
about 1$\frac{1}{2}$ pints mussels · seasoning · parsley ·
1–1$\frac{1}{2}$ lb diced raw young chicken ·
7 oz. long grain rice ·
approximately 8 oz. shelled prawns · few cooked peas**

Blend the saffron powder with the stock, or infuse the strands for 30 minutes, then strain. Heat the oil in a large pan and fry the chopped onions and crushed garlic for a few minutes. Meanwhile put the washed mussels into another pan with enough water to cover. Discard any mussels that do not close when sharply tapped. Add seasoning and a bunch of parsley. Heat until the mussels open. Allow to cool enough to handle, remove most of the mussels from *both* shells, but save a few on halved shells. Add the diced chicken and rice to the onions and garlic, toss in the oily mixture and pour in the saffron flavoured stock. Simmer steadily in an uncovered pan, stirring from time to time, until the rice is almost tender (about 25 minutes). Add the prawns, peas, mussels and seasoning and complete the cooking.

To vary: Fry 2 skinned, chopped tomatoes with the onion.

APRICOT LEMON SOUFFLE

**1 large can apricot halves · juice 2 lemons ·
1 oz. powdered gelatine (enough to set 2 pints) ·
5 eggs · 3 oz. caster sugar* · $\frac{3}{4}$ pint thick cream ·
chocolate vermicelli**
*little more if wished

Tie a deep band of buttered greaseproof paper round the outside of the soufflé dish.

Drain the fruit from the syrup, put 8 halves on one side for decoration. Sieve (or emulsify) the rest of the fruit, add the lemon juice and enough syrup to give $\frac{3}{4}$ pint. Soften the gelatine in a little of the cold apricot mixture. Heat the remainder, stir the softened gelatine into this, and continue stirring until thoroughly dissolved. Beat the egg yolks with the sugar, then whisk in the warm apricot mixture. Allow this mixture to cool and begin to stiffen slightly then fold in $\frac{1}{2}$ pint whipped cream and the stiffly beaten egg whites. Spoon into the prepared soufflé dish and leave to set. Remove the band of paper from the mixture and press chocolate vermicelli against the sides. Top with piped thick cream and the reserved apricots.

Suggested Wines

Serve a dry sherry, dry white wine or hock with the hors d'oeuvre. A red wine is ideal with the Paella – choose a Chateau d'Arche or a Spanish Villa Zaco (this is a claret type wine).

Mixed Hors d'Oeuvre, Paella, Apricot Lemon Soufflé

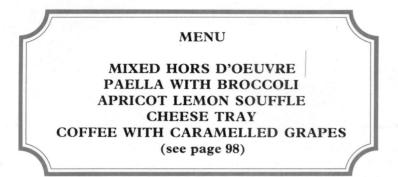

MENU

**MIXED HORS D'OEUVRE
PAELLA WITH BROCCOLI
APRICOT LEMON SOUFFLE
CHEESE TRAY
COFFEE WITH CARAMELLED GRAPES**
(see page 98)

Here is a menu for a celebration dinner. The menu is planned for 6 people, but would serve 8.

Advance Preparations: A mixed hors d'oeuvre is an excellent start to a meal. It looks colourful, can be prepared beforehand and allows guests to select the items they prefer. Mix the oil and vinegar dressing and use as required.

Many people have enjoyed Paella in Spain and would be delighted to have it again, so it is a clever choice. It can be partially cooked earlier.

The cold Apricot Lemon Soufflé has a sharp refreshing taste which contrasts with the previous courses. There is no need to have a wide range of cheeses after such a satisfying meal, one or two would be quite sufficient.

Bunches of caramelled grapes are delicious with the coffee (see page 98).

Preparation of Paella

MIXED HORS D'OEUVRE

Salami Cornets: Twist 12 slices of salami into cones. Slice about 12 small white raw button mushrooms, toss in oil and vinegar, season well. Spoon into the cones, top with halved stuffed olives. Alternatively pipe rosettes of thick mayonnaise and top with olives.

Red Pepper and Cucumber Salad: Blend 3–4 tablespoons diced cucumber with 3–4 tablespoons diced canned red pepper. Toss in well seasoned oil and vinegar.

Carrot Creamed Coleslaw: Blend a little cream and lemon juice into about 3 tablespoons mayonnaise. Toss 5–6 tablespoons shredded white cabbage and the same amount of coarsely grated carrot with the dressing.

Tomato and Onion Salad: Blend oil and vinegar with seasoning and a pinch of sugar. Cut 1 large onion and

MENU

TOMATO AND CELERY SOUP
BEEF SPIRALS WITH PEAS,
CARROTS AND WATERCRESS
APPLE RAISIN MOULD
AND ICE CREAM OR YOGHOURT

A celebration menu need not be unduly expensive. This menu, for 4 people, is economical and easily prepared. It is also excellent for the 'calorie-conscious'.

Advance Preparations: Make the soup ready to reheat, or serve chilled. Prepare the Beef Spirals, cover until ready to cook, so the meat does not dry.

Make the dessert and allow to set; do not keep this longer than 24 hours, otherwise it becomes too stiff.

TOMATO AND CELERY SOUP

**2 medium-sized onions · 3–4 sticks celery ·
1 oz. margarine · 1 lb. tomatoes · $\frac{1}{2}$ pint white stock ·
seasoning · 1 tablespoon concentrated tomato purée ·
Garnish: celery leaves**

Chop the onions and celery. Toss in the margarine for a few minutes. Add the chopped tomatoes and stock and simmer for 15 minutes. Sieve or emulsify. Return to the pan, heat for a few minutes, then add the seasoning and tomato purée. Pour into soup cups or a tureen. Garnish with chopped celery leaves. This soup is also excellent cold.

BEEF SPIRALS

**generous 1 lb. rump steak cut in one piece ·
3 oz. butter or margarine ·
2–3 tablespoons chopped parsley and/or 1 finely chopped green or red pepper · peas · sliced carrots ·**

Beat the steak until thin. Spread with half the butter or margarine then the chopped parsley and/or the chopped pepper (discard the core and seeds). Roll like a Swiss roll, cut into 8 slices and secure the spirals with wooden cocktail sticks. Grill or fry in the rest of the butter or margarine until tender. Serve in a border of peas and sliced carrots.

APPLE RAISIN MOULD

**2 good-sized cooking apples · $\frac{1}{2}$ pint water ·
grated rind and juice 1 orange · sugar to taste ·
$\frac{1}{2}$ oz. powdered gelatine (or enough to set 1 pint).
2–3 tablespoons seedless raisins ·
Decoration: fresh orange slices**

Simmer the peeled and cored apples with the water, finely grated rind of the orange and sugar to taste. Beat, sieve or emulsify until smooth. Soften the powdered gelatine in the cold orange juice. Measure the apple pulp and you should have *nearly* 1 pint; if insufficient add a little hot water to make the correct amount. Blend the gelatine with the hot apple purée and stir until dissolved. Put the raisins into the bottom of a mould rinsed out in cold water. Spoon the apple mixture over these. Leave to set. Turn out, decorate with fresh orange slices and serve with ice cream or yoghourt.

Suggested Wines
Choose a Red Burgundy for this menu or a dry cider.

Tomato and Celery Soup

Simple Celebration Cake

MENU

**OPEN SANDWICHES
SIMPLE CELEBRATION CAKE
SHERRY OR CHAMPAGNE
AND/OR
TEA OR COFFEE**

Sometimes one wants a very simple Celebration menu; to invite a few friends to 'drop in' for a drink and cake.

Advance Preparations: Cut thin slices of bread and butter, either brown or white, and top with smoked salmon; pâté, topped with crisply grilled bacon; inexpensive Danish caviare, topped with hard-boiled egg slices; lightly scrambled egg, topped with prawns; smoked eel sprinkled with lemon juice; crab meat mashed with mayonnaise and sprinkled with paprika. Cut into small pieces and cover with damp kitchen paper or foil. Make the Celebration Cake 24 hours beforehand.

SIMPLE CELEBRATION CAKE

**Victoria sandwich mixture: 8 oz. margarine or butter ·
8 oz. caster sugar · 4 eggs ·
8 oz. self-raising flour or plain flour and 2 teaspoons baking powder ·
Icing: 12 oz. butter or margarine · 1½ lb. icing sugar ·
finely grated rind 1 orange ·
about 3 tablespoons orange juice ·
few drops yellow or pink colouring**

Cream the margarine or butter with the sugar until soft and light. Add the beaten eggs gradually and then fold in the sieved flour or flour and baking powder. Divide the mixture between two greased and floured 8–9-inch sandwich tins and bake for approximately 25–30 minutes above the centre of a moderate oven, 350–375°F., Gas Mark 4–5. Turn out carefully and cool. Prepare the icing by creaming the butter or margarine, icing sugar, orange rind and juice and colouring. Sandwich the cakes together with one quarter of the icing. Coat the sides and top with some of the icing, then tint the remaining icing a slightly deeper colour and pipe over the top of the cake. Decorate with a ribbon and candles or a few flowers. Makes 16 small slices.

Gazpacho Garnishes, Ham and Tongue Loaf with Corn Salad, Chocolate Macaroon Trifle

MENU

GAZPACHO
HAM AND TONGUE LOAF
WITH CORN SALAD
CHOCOLATE MACAROON TRIFLE

This menu is an economical one which would be ideal to serve for a formal or buffet meal.

Advance Preparations: All the dishes are prepared beforehand and served cold. Cover the salad with foil, so it does not dry.

GAZPACHO

There are many recipes for this excellent chilled tomato and vegetable soup from Spain.

1 pint canned tomato juice ·
1 tablespoon lemon juice · 2 tablespoons olive oil ·
1–2 crushed cloves garlic · 1 onion · seasoning ·
Garnish: finely diced cucumber ·
finely diced green pepper · finely diced onion ·
finely diced bread

Blend the tomato juice, lemon juice, olive oil, garlic and finely chopped onion. Season and chill. Serve with the 4 bowls of garnish.

HAM AND TONGUE LOAF

8 oz. tongue* · 12 oz. boiled bacon or ham ·
2 oz. soft breadcrumbs ·
4 tablespoons sieved or emulsified fresh tomato pulp ·
1–2 tablespoons chopped parsley · 1 egg · seasoning
Garnish: sliced radishes and cucumber

lambs' tongues are always cheaper than ox tongue

Mince or chop the tongue with the boiled bacon or ham (try to buy *pieces* of cooked ham). Add the breadcrumbs, tomato pulp, chopped parsley, egg and seasoning. Grease a 2-lb. loaf tin, put in the ham and tongue mixture. Cover with greased foil and bake in the centre of a moderate oven, 350–375°F., Gas Mark 4–5, for about 1 hour. Cool in the tin. Turn out, garnish and serve with corn salad.

CORN SALAD

about 8 oz. cooked or canned sweet corn · lettuce · 3 hard boiled eggs · 6–8 cold new potatoes · little mayonnaise · chopped parsley

Put cooked or canned corn on a bed of lettuce. Garnish with quartered hard boiled eggs and sliced potatoes. Top with mayonnaise and chopped parsley.

CHOCOLATE MACAROON TRIFLE

6–8 macaroon biscuits · 2 tablespoons rum · 3 tablespoons fresh orange juice · 1 oz. cornflour · ¾ pint milk · 2 oz. sugar · 4–6 oz. plain chocolate · ¼ pint thick cream · Topping: whipped cream · few blanched almonds

Put the macaroon biscuits into a serving dish. Blend the rum with the fresh orange juice. Pour over the biscuits. Blend the cornflour with the milk. Cook gently until thickened, with the sugar. Remove from the heat and add the chocolate, broken into small pieces, stir until dissolved. Stir as the sauce cools and blend with the thick cream. Pour over the biscuits and leave until fairly firm. Top with whipped cream and blanched almonds.

Suggested Wines

Serve a well chilled white Bordeaux (Graves is a good choice).

```
┌─────────────────────────────────┐
│              MENU               │
│                                 │
│        CHEESE AIGRETTES         │
│   TROUT NANSEN WITH CUCUMBER    │
│  SALAD, ASPARAGUS AND NEW POTATOES │
│         PACIFIC DELIGHT         │
└─────────────────────────────────┘
```

Although the main course and the dessert may appear rather ambitious, they are both simple to prepare. This is a frankly luxurious luncheon for 4.

Advance Preparations: I have suggested hot Cheese Aigrettes since the main course is cold and the dessert a combination of hot and cold ingredients. If you do not wish to fry these at the last minute, serve a hot soup, or a pâté, or hot globe artichokes with melted butter (in this case choose another vegetable, *not* asparagus). Prepare the ingredients for the aigrettes; cut the skin from the pineapple and make the main course completely. Make the cucumber salad and cover, prepare the asparagus.

CHEESE AIGRETTES

**1 oz. butter or margarine · 3 tablespoons water ·
2 oz. flour, preferably plain · 2 large eggs ·
1½ oz. grated Parmesan cheese · seasoning ·
To fry: deep oil ·
Garnish (optional): grated Parmesan, or Parmesan
and Cheddar cheese or flaked almonds**

Put the butter or margarine with the water into a pan. Heat until the butter or margarine has melted, remove from the heat and stir in the flour. Return to the heat and cook gently for several minutes, until a firm ball. Again remove from the heat and gradually beat in the eggs until a smooth sticky mixture. Add the cheese (do not replace over the heat), season well. Heat the oil to 350°F. (until a tiny piece of the mixture turns golden coloured within about a minute). Drop spoonfuls of the mixture into the hot oil, lower the heat and cook for about 7 minutes, turning during cooking. Drain well on absorbent paper. Sprinkle with the garnish if wished. Makes about 16–20.
Note These can be fried, put on a flat tray in a low oven and kept hot for a *very limited time only*.

TROUT NANSEN

**4 large trout · little seasoning ·
½ pint white wine or use half wine and half water ·
¼ pint fish stock* · bouquet garni ·
enough aspic jelly powder to set ½ pint ·
2–3 tablespoons thick mayonnaise ·
little chopped parsley · 2–3 teaspoons chopped capers ·
1 tablespoon chopped gherkins ·
Garnish: 2 lemons · shelled prawns or shrimps ·
2 tomatoes ·
little cooked or canned asparagus · parsley**
*made by simmering the back bones for a short time or by simmering a small cod's head

Slit the trout along the stomach and carefully remove the backbones (or ask the fishmonger to do this). If using frozen trout allow to defrost, then bone. Try to leave the heads on

Cheese Aigrettes, Trout Nansen, Pacific Delight

the fish as shown in the picture. Wash and dry the fish well, season *very* lightly. Put into a large pan with the wine or wine and water and fish stock. Add the *bouquet garni*, but no more seasoning. Simmer very gently until tender, i.e. about 8–10 minutes. Lift the fish out of the liquid and drain well.
Strain the liquid most carefully, measure and if necessary add a little more wine or water to give just *over* ½ pint. Soften the aspic jelly powder in a little of the liquid, heat the rest, then add the softened aspic jelly, stir until dissolved. Put on one side and leave until cool and beginning to stiffen. Meanwhile blend the mayonnaise, parsley, capers and gherkins and spread a little inside each fish. Put the fish on a serving dish with the sliced lemons and the prawns or shrimps. Peel the tomatoes, slice and cut one or two slices into small pieces, put these on the lemon slices. Arrange the rest of the sliced tomatoes and asparagus on the dish, as shown in the picture. Spoon the cold and slightly stiffened jelly over the fish and garnish and leave until set. Top with parsley.

Cucumber Salad

Peel the cucumber if wished and slice thinly. Top with a little seasoning, lemon juice or white wine vinegar and chopped parsley and chopped chives.

Asparagus

Cut the ends from the asparagus, wash in cold water, tie in bundles and stand in boiling salted water. If you have no asparagus-boiler use the tallest pan possible (I find a deep pressure cooker, used as an ordinary saucepan, excellent). Put a lid on the pan, or cover with foil to retain the steam. Cook for about 20–25 minutes, until tender. Drain and serve with well seasoned melted butter.

PACIFIC DELIGHT

**1 ripe medium-sized pineapple ·
ice cream to serve 4 ·
Meringue: 4 egg whites · 4 oz. caster sugar**

Cut the top from the pineapple very carefully. Put on one side to use for decoration. Cut the pineapple into rings, remove the skin from each slice with a sharp knife or kitchen scissors. Take out the centre core with an apple corer. Whisk the egg whites until very stiff. Gradually whisk in half the sugar then fold in the remainder. Put the first slice of pineapple on to an oven-proof serving dish. Fill the centre 'hole' with firm ice cream. Top with a second slice of fruit and ice cream, continue like this until the fruit is put together. Put the meringue mixture into a cloth piping bag with a ¼-inch rose, and pipe to look like the original shape of the pineapple. Put into a very hot oven, 475–500°F., Gas Mark 8–9 and leave for 3 minutes only, until the meringue is tinged with golden brown. Remove from the oven. Put the leaves on top of the meringue shape and serve. This dessert will stand for 25–30 minutes without the ice cream melting.
Note When fresh pineapple is not available, use rings of well drained canned pineapple, in which case use a little less sugar in the meringue.
There is another way to serve this dessert, and that is to peel the pineapple and cut it into slices downwards, removing the hard core. Put a block of ice cream on to the dish, press the slices against the ice cream so it looks like a whole pineapple again, then coat with meringue as the recipe above.

Suggested Wines

A well chilled white wine or rosé would blend well with this menu.

This menu is ideal for a hot weather buffet served in the garden. It serves 10–12.

Advance Preparations: All the dishes are made beforehand.

CHILLED CHICKEN CREAM SOUP

2 pints chicken stock · 2–3 onions or leeks · 2–3 old potatoes · *bouquet garni* **· seasoning · about 8 oz. cooked chicken breast · ½ pint thin cream · chopped chives · chopped parsley**

Put the stock into a pan, add the onions or leeks, potatoes and *bouquet garni* with some seasoning. Simmer for about 20 minutes. Add the chicken and continue cooking for a further 10 minutes. Remove the *bouquet garni*, then sieve, or emulsify the mixture in a liquidiser. Add the cream, more seasoning and a generous amount of chives and parsley. Serve very cold.

BEEF AND HAM PATE LOAF

1½ lb. rump steak · 8–12 oz. calf's liver · 1 lb. cooked ham · 2 oz. butter or margarine · 2 oz. flour · ¼ pint brown stock · ½ pint milk · 4–5 tablespoons thick cream · 2–3 tablespoons dry sherry · 5 eggs · seasoning · 1–2 teaspoons chopped fresh herbs

Mince the steak, liver and ham very finely. Make a fairly thick sauce with the butter or margarine, flour, stock and milk. Add the cream, sherry, 2 beaten eggs, plenty of seasoning and the herbs. Add all the meats and blend well. Hard boil the 3 remaining eggs, shell. Put half the meat mixture into a large 3–4-pint buttered mould, arrange the eggs on this, cover with the rest of the meat mixture, then with well buttered foil or greaseproof paper. Stand in a tin of cold water and bake for 1½ hours in the centre of a very moderate oven, 325°F., Gas Mark 3. Cool in the tin, then turn out just before serving. Serve with salads and mayonnaise.

SPONGE FINGER GATEAU

about 30 sponge fingers · 1 pint thick cream · sugar to taste · 1½–2 lb. fresh fruit

Put one-third of the sponge fingers on a serving dish. Whip the cream, add sugar to taste. Spread some of the cream over the sponge fingers, top with some of the fruit. Add more sponge fingers, more cream and fruit, then a final layer of sponge fingers, cream and fruit. Allow to stand for 1–2 hours before serving.

To vary: Dip the sponge fingers in a little white wine for a few seconds only.

Suggested Wines
Chianti or a light white wine such as a hock.

A buffet party menu which would be ideal for hot or cold weather. It serves 10–12 people. If you wanted to serve an hors d'oeuvre, the Creamed Liver Pâté on page 91 would be a good choice.

Advance Preparations: Coat the scampi and chicken; make the sauces, dessert and cheese savouries. The cheese savouries can be made several days before and stored in an airtight tin.

FRIED SCAMPI AND FRIED CHICKEN

These two fried foods may be served together, or can be served separately. If you do not know your guests tastes, it is a good idea to serve them separately as quite a number of people are allergic to shell fish. For a buffet party, cut the chicken into small pieces and removes bones and the skin. Allow 4 scampi per person plus about 2–3 small pieces of chicken. For about 48 scampi and 36 pieces of chicken you will need:

1 lb. flour, preferably plain · seasoning · 4 eggs · 1 pint milk · nearly ½ pint water · 3–4 oz. well seasoned flour

Make a batter with the flour, seasoning, eggs, milk and water. Coat the fish and the chicken in seasoned flour, then in batter. Fry scampi in deep fat for about 2–3 minutes, and chicken about 6–8 minutes. Drain on absorbent paper and serve hot. Obviously if you are frying as large an amount as that suggested above, you will have to keep it warm, so place on flat trays in a low oven.

OLIVE TARTARE SAUCE

2–3 tablespoons chopped gherkins · 2–3 tablespoons capers · 2–3 tablespoons chopped parsley · 2–3 tablespoons sliced stuffed olives · ½ pint mayonnaise · little lemon juice · seasoning

Mix the gherkins, capers, parsley and olives with the mayonnaise. Add the lemon juice and extra seasoning.

SPICED PICKLED CUCUMBER SAUCE

small jar pickled cucumbers · 1–2 teaspoons peppercorns · little mixed spice · 1–2 teaspoons made mustard

Chop or slice the cucumbers. Blend the peppercorns, spice and mustard with the liquid from the jar of cucumbers. Put the cucumbers into a dish, pour the spiced liquid over these.

HERBED CHUTNEY
Take any sweet chutney, mango, tomato, etc. and blend with finely chopped parsley, chives and any other fresh herbs.

Chilled Chicken Cream Soup, Beef and Ham Pâté Loaf, Salads, Sponge Finger Gâteau

CAPSICUM SAUCE

**1–2 medium-sized green peppers · 1–2 red peppers ·
2 tablespoons olive oil ·
2–3 tablespoons white malt or wine vinegar ·
1 teaspoon made mustard · 1 teaspoon sugar ·
1–2 teaspoons peppercorns or very good shake black
pepper and salt ·
1–2 tablespoons sultanas or raisins (optional)**

Chop the green and red peppers and blend together. Discard
the cores and seeds and use canned red peppers if the fresh
are not available. Blend the olive oil, vinegar, mustard,
sugar and peppercorns or pepper and salt. Pour over the cap-
sicums and allow to stand for about 1 hour. Add the sultanas
or raisins if wished.

ORANGES IN RUM SAUCE

**12 medium-sized oranges · ½ pint water ·
8 oz. granulated sugar · 4–5 tablespoons rum**

Cut away the peel from the oranges, so you remove all the
pith as well. Cut the orange part of some of the peel into
very narrow strips, as shown in the picture. Soak in half
the water for 1 hour, then simmer in this water in a covered
pan for about 20 minutes. Stand in the liquid until ready to
add this to the caramel. Put the sugar and the remainder of
the water into a strong pan. Stir over a low heat until the
sugar dissolves, then boil steadily, without stirring, until the
mixture turns golden brown. Strain the liquid from the orange
peel into the caramel, stir over the heat until blended, then
add the rum. Put the oranges into a dish, pour the syrup over
slowly so it soaks into the fruit and top with the peel.

PARTY PUNCH

**2 bottles rosé wine · about 1 pint soda water ·
2 glasses brandy**

Blend the wine with the soda water and brandy. *If wishing
to serve as a hot punch:* Heat with 2–3 tablespoons sugar and
the juice of 1–2 lemons. Top with lemon slices. *If wishing to
serve cold:* I do not add sugar or lemon juice, but just pour
the wine, soda and brandy mixture over a little crushed ice
and decorate with slices of lemon and mint. *Gives about
12–16 glasses.*

Oranges in Rum Sauce

This menu would be of special appeal to young people. It serves 10–12.

Advance Preparations: Make the dip and prepare the tray of foods around the dip. Partially cook the Kedgeree and just reheat; prepare the Shish-Kebabs.

AVOCADO DIP (GUACAMOLE)

2 large avocado pears · 3 large tomatoes · 1 small onion · $\frac{1}{4}$ pint soured cream · 1 tablespoon lemon juice · 3 tablespoons mayonnaise · seasoning · few drops Tabasco sauce

Halve the pears, remove the flesh and mash. Add the remaining ingredients. Serve with crisps, raw vegetables and biscuits.

KEDGEREE

4 oz. butter or margarine · 1 lb. cooked rice · 1$\frac{1}{2}$ lb. cooked smoked haddock · $\frac{1}{4}$ pint thin cream · 3–4 hard boiled eggs · seasoning

Heat the butter or margarine in a pan. Add the rice, the flaked haddock and cream. Heat gently, then add the chopped egg whites and seasoning. Top with the chopped egg yolks.

SHISH-KEBABS

Put cubes of tender lamb, rolled in seasoning and a little chopped fresh rosemary on to metal skewers, with rings of courgette or cucumber and/or rings of green pepper and/or slices of lemon. You can also add small mushrooms, tomatoes and tiny onions (par-boil these first). Brush with oil or melted butter and grill until tender. Serve with various sauces; those on page 108 would be excellent.

Suggested Drinks: Cider or beer or soft drinks.

Avocado Dip (Guacamole)

MENU

SEAFOOD SCALLOPS
CYPRUS CHICKEN SALAD IN RICE RING
CHESTNUT AND RUM SWISS GATEAU
CHEESE TRAY

This menu serves 6–8

Advance Preparations: Make and bake the pastry and make the filling and garnish for the Seafood Scallops. Prepare ingredients for the salad and make gâteau. Arrange the cheese tray.

Seafood Scallops

SEAFOOD SCALLOPS

short crust pastry made with 8–10 oz. flour, etc. ·
(see page 70) ·
Filling: 2 oz. butter or margarine · 2 oz. flour ·
¾ pint milk · 1 small onion · *bouquet garni* ·
seasoning · 2–3 tablespoons thick cream ·
2 egg yolks · 1 small canned red pepper ·
8–12 oz. cooked white fish · 8 oz. shell fish ·
1–2 tablespoons dry sherry ·
Garnish: 1 oz. butter · 1–2 rashers lean bacon ·
few mushrooms · parsley

Roll out the pastry and line 6 or 8 large patty tins or scallop shells. If the scallop shells are rather large you need the 10 oz. flour. Bake 'blind' for about 15 minutes until crisp and golden brown above the centre of a hot oven, 425–450°F., Gas Mark 6–7. To make the filling, heat the butter, stir the flour into this and cook for several minutes. Gradually blend in the milk, add the onion and herbs, bring to the boil and cook until a thick sauce. Remove onion and herbs and whisk the sauce sharply. *Heat gently* again, add seasoning, the cream blended with the egg yolks, the chopped red pepper, flaked fish, shell fish and sherry. *If serving hot:* Put the *hot* filling into the *hot* pastry cases, top with the garnish and serve. *If serving cold:* Allow the pastry to cool, and also the filling.

Put the cold filling into the cold pastry and top with the garnish. To prepare the garnish, heat the butter and fry the chopped bacon and the sliced mushrooms.

CYPRUS CHICKEN SALAD IN RICE RING

Rice ring: 7 oz. long grain rice ·
1 pint very well clarified chicken stock ·
¼ pint fresh orange juice · seasoning ·
2–3 tablespoons olive oil ·
1–1½ tablespoons white wine vinegar ·
Garnish: finely shredded peel 2–3 oranges ·
Chicken salad: 5 lb. cooked chicken ·
¼ pint mayonnaise · about 3–4 tablespoons white wine ·
1 tablespoon olive oil · seasoning · 1 green pepper ·
1–2 teaspoons freshly chopped herbs ·
about 8 oz. grapes · 2–4 tablespoons blanched almonds

Put the washed rice into a pan with the stock, orange juice and seasoning. Bring to the boil, lower the heat, cover the pan and simmer gently for about 15 minutes until the rice is just tender and the liquid has evaporated.

While the rice is cooking, blend the oil and vinegar and soak the shredded peel in this to soften. Drain the peel well, then blend enough oil and vinegar into the rice, with extra seasoning, to make it slightly moistened and full of flavour. Form into a ring on the serving dish, allow to cool, then top with the orange peel. To make the salad, cut the meat from the bones, save some of the very best pieces of breast for the top garnish. Blend the mayonnaise with the white wine and oil, season well. The dressing should have a slightly sharp flavour. Cut the green pepper into neat pieces, discarding the core and seeds. Blend the diced chicken, pepper and herbs into the dressing, pile into the centre of the rice ring. Garnish with the reserved chicken breast, grapes and the browned almonds.

CHESTNUT AND RUM SWISS GATEAU

For the cake: 3 large eggs · 4 oz. caster sugar ·
3 oz. flour, plain or self-raising · 2 oz. butter ·
little extra caster sugar ·
Filling: small can unsweetened chestnut purée ·
1 egg yolk · 4 oz. sieved icing sugar ·
1–2 tablespoons rum ·
Coating: 1 egg white · 10 oz. sieved icing sugar ·
little warm water · 2–3 oz. plain chocolate

Whisk the eggs and sugar until thick. Sieve the flour, melt and cool the butter. Fold the flour, then the butter into the egg and sugar mixture. Pour into a Swiss roll tin lined with well greased greaseproof paper. Bake for approximately 12–15 minutes just above the centre of a moderate to moderately hot oven, 375–400°F., Gas Mark 5–6. Turn on to sugared paper, roll round the paper and allow to cool.

Blend the chestnut purée with the egg yolk, icing sugar and enough rum to give a soft creamy-like filling. Unroll the cold sponge, spread with the filling and re-roll. Whisk the egg white lightly, add the icing sugar and enough water to give an icing soft enough to flow. Smooth over the roll and 'swirl' slightly, then leave to set. Melt the chocolate in a basin over hot, but not boiling, water. Arrange several well washed and dried leaves on a flat dish, spread the melted chocolate over these, allow to set. Lift the chocolate off the leaves carefully and arrange on top of the cake.

Suggested Wines: A really well chilled Chablis.

Cyprus Chicken Salad in Rice Ring, Chestnut and Rum Swiss Gâteau

One of the easiest, and most enjoyable, of buffet-type parties is to serve a variety of cheeses with suitable wines.

If you are expecting rather a large number of guests and have relatively little space in which to entertain them, dice the cheese beforehand, so it is easier to serve. The cheese looks more inviting, in this case, if the cubes are placed on cocktail sticks and speared into red and/or green cabbages and grapefruit. Obviously cheese that crumbles easily, such as mature Danish Blue and Roquefort, cannot be served in this way, and should be arranged in bowls or on dishes with colourful garnishes. The usual arrangement, though, is to have several cheese boards on the table, each one containing a selection of cheese and garnished with bunches of grapes, orange segments, radishes, celery, etc., so your guests may then help themselves.

Cheeses to Choose

It is wise to 'play for safety' by having some well known, also much liked, Cheddar cheese. If you have this, then choose either Cheshire or Double Gloucester as a second firm cheese. Have a full flavoured cheese, such as Danish Blue, Roquefort, Stilton, or Gorgonzola.

Choose a 'creamy' type cheese with plenty of flavour such as a Brie or Camembert or Pont l'Eveque and a really creamy cheese such as Bel Paese, or a local cream cheese.

Many people today are calorie-conscious so have bowls of low-calorie cottage cheese. As this is very colourless you may like to mix it with chopped herbs or chopped fresh fruit.

The above are the basic ideas; there is such a variety of cheeses from which to choose that your Cheese Party need never be dull.

Some extra cheeses I personally would include would be a Smoked cheese, a Port du Salut, a very good Caerphilly and a Sage Derby (Derby cheese with the flavour of fresh sage), plus garlic-flavoured cream cheese. If your party includes children then the milder processed cheeses might well be popular.

The suggested wines are given below. If you wish to provide

just a choice of one red, and one white or rosé (and this is certainly easier for serving), then I would choose the wines that come at the beginning of the lists. On the other hand it is enjoyable for your guests to sample a variety of wines on such an occasion.

Suggested Wines

Red Wines

Mouton-Rothschild or Mouton-Cadet, Médoc, St. Emilion, Nuits St. Georges, Gevrey-Chambertin, Volnay, or an Italian Valpolicella.

White Wines

Pouilly-Fuissé or better still if you like an interesting flavour, a Pouilly Fumée, Puligny-Montrachet or some of the German Hocks – Liebfraumilch is one of the most popular. Try also a Riesling or a Soave di Verona from Italy.

Rosé Wines

The best known Portuguese Mateus Rosé blends well with many cheeses, but less hackneyed is the French Tavel rosé or Beaujolais rosé or a really dry Pradei rosé or even an Anjou rosé.

Many people might enjoy a beer or lager or cider with the cheese.

Serve white and rosé wines well chilled, red wines at room temperature.

Some of the best accompaniments to cheese will be crusty French bread or crisp rolls. Have crispbreads, various biscuits and fingers of a rich fruit cake (or tiny hot mince pies) to blend with the creamy cheese. Include plenty of salads and fruit too. The fruits I would choose would be fingers of ripe melon, crisp apples, firm, but ripe pears and cherries when in season.

Quantities to Allow

Allow 6–8 oz. cheese per person – buy generously, for the cheese will keep – and 3 rolls or the equivalent in bread with several biscuits or crispbreads per person plus about 2 oz. butter per person.

If you allow $\frac{1}{2}$ bottle of wine per person that should be sufficient.

Coffee will also be appreciated so allow 2 cups of coffee per person.

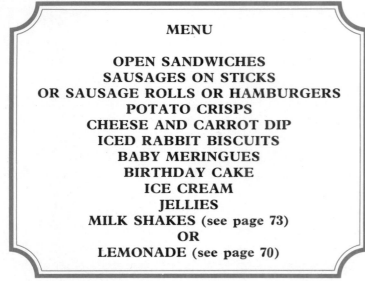

MENU

OPEN SANDWICHES
SAUSAGES ON STICKS
OR SAUSAGE ROLLS OR HAMBURGERS
POTATO CRISPS
CHEESE AND CARROT DIP
ICED RABBIT BISCUITS
BABY MERINGUES
BIRTHDAY CAKE
ICE CREAM
JELLIES
MILK SHAKES (see page 73)
OR
LEMONADE (see page 70)

Advance Preparations: All the food can be prepared in advance. The sausage rolls and hamburgers can just be reheated.

OPEN SANDWICHES

bridge rolls · butter or margarine ·
toppings (see method)

Split the rolls, spread with butter and then with the topping:

SAVOURY TOPPINGS:

Scrambled eggs; cream cheese spread (or a not too rich cream cheese); yeast extract; ham; potted meat and potted fish. Garnish with cooked well drained prunes, mandarin orange segments or tomato slices.

SWEET TOPPINGS:

Mashed banana (with a little sugar and lemon juice); honey; jam; peanut butter and nuts. Decorate with prunes, halved dates or apple slices.

SAUSAGES ON STICKS

If you cannot buy small cocktail sausages twist chipolata

sausages in half and then cut through to give 2 sausages. Grill, fry or bake in the oven until brown; drain on absorbent paper. Reheat as required or serve cold.

CHEESE AND CARROT DIP

1 lb. Cheddar cheese · nearly $\frac{1}{4}$ pint top of the milk ·
1–2 tablespoons mayonnaise · 2–3 firm carrots

Grate the cheese finely and blend with enough top of the milk to make a consistency like thick cream, then add a little mayonnaise to make a more piquant flavour. Grate the carrots finely, stir most of the carrot into the cheese mixture. Spoon into a dish and top with the rest of the carrot. Serve on a large plate with potato crisps and sausages as 'dips'. Serves about 12.

ICED RABBIT BISCUITS

6 oz. margarine · 6 oz. caster sugar ·
12 oz. flour, preferably plain · little milk or egg ·
Decoration: 8 oz. icing sugar · little orange juice ·
colouring · currants

Cream the margarine and sugar, add the flour and just enough milk or egg to make a firm rolling consistency. Knead well, roll out on a lightly floured board and cut into 'rabbit' shapes, either using a metal cutter or cutting round a cardboard shape. Save enough dough to cut oblong pieces, upon which the 'rabbits' will stand when baked or baked and iced. Put on to ungreased baking trays, bake for 12–15 minutes in the centre of a very moderate oven, 325–350°F., Gas Mark 3–4. Cool on the trays and store until ready to serve. Blend the icing sugar with orange juice and colouring, ice the 'stands' and the 'rabbits', press currants in position for 'eyes'. The biscuits may be served without icing. Makes about 16.

SAUSAGE ROLLS

Flaky pastry: 1 lb. flour, preferably plain ·
pinch salt ·
12 oz. margarine or a mixture of margarine and fat
or butter · water to bind · 1$\frac{1}{2}$ lb. sausagemeat · 2 eggs

Flaky pastry is better for children, as it is less rich than puff pastry. Sieve the flour and salt, rub in one-third of the

Cheese and Carrot Dip, Iced Rabbit Biscuits, Baby Meringues, Open Sandwiches, Birthday Cake

Hamburgers

margarine or mixed fats and bind with water to an elastic rolling consistency. Roll out to an oblong shape. Divide the remaining fat into half, then into tiny pieces. Cover two-thirds of the dough with half the fat, fold like an envelope, turn at right angles, seal the edges, 'rib' the pastry (i.e. depress at regular intervals). Roll out and repeat with the rest of the fat, fold, turn at right angles, seal the edges and put into a cool place until ready to use.

Make the sausagemeat into long strips, about the thickness of a large cigar. Roll out the pastry and cut into strips, sufficiently wide to cover the sausagemeat. Put the strips of sausagemeat on to the strips of pastry. Brush the edges with water, seal firmly and flake with the edge of a knife. Cut into pieces about 1½ inches in length and, make 2–3 slits on top. Beat the eggs with a little water, brush over the sausage rolls and bake on ungreased baking trays for about 12 minutes in the centre of a very hot oven, 450–475°F., Gas Mark 7–8, then lower the heat to moderate and cook for another 5–6 minutes. Serve hot or cold. Makes 36 rolls – allow 2–3 per person.

HAMBURGERS

**2 lb. minced rump or other good quality beef ·
2 eggs or 4 egg yolks · seasoning ·
pinch mixed herbs · flour · fat for frying · rolls**

Mix the meat, eggs or egg yolks, seasoning and herbs together and form into about 24 small flat cakes. If you flour your hands you can handle the meat mixture more easily. Fry in a little hot fat for about 3 minutes on either side or bake on well greased baking trays for about 12 minutes in a hot oven. Serve on small toasted round rolls. Makes about 24.

BABY MERINGUES

**White meringues: 2 egg whites · 4 oz. caster sugar ·
Chocolate meringues: 2 egg whites ·
4 oz. caster sugar ·
2 level tablespoons chocolate powder**

Whisk the egg whites until stiff. Beat in half the sugar then fold in the remainder. When making the chocolate meringues blend the chocolate powder with the sugar. Pipe into rose shapes on lightly oiled baking trays and dry out for approximately 1½ hours in the coolest part of a very slow oven, 250–275°F., Gas Mark 0–½. Lift off the baking trays while warm, cool then store in an airtight tin until ready to serve. They can be served plain or sandwiched together with whipped cream. This makes about 36.

BIRTHDAY CAKE

Make a Victoria sandwich (see page 103), using 8 oz. margarine etc., then sandwich together and decorate with butter icing and with a chocolate figure as in the picture. Tie a band of ribbon round the outside of the cake. This makes about 14–16 slices.

NEW WAYS TO SERVE JELLIES

Make up fruit flavoured jellies and:
Whisk and fill ice cream cones.
Whisk and put on to saucers, top with pear 'mice'.
Cut a slice from oranges, squeeze out the juice and use this to make the jelly (adding water to bring up to the full quantity). Remove the pith and fill the orange cases with the cool jelly. When set put the 'lids' into position.

Cocktail Parties

This is an ideal way to entertain a large number of people, either at mid-day or early in the evening. The drinks can be as varied as you wish. The food can be simple or original and hot or cold. A good selection of cocktail savouries should look gay and colourful.

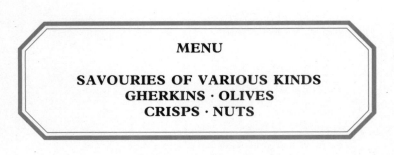

```
MENU

SAVOURIES OF VARIOUS KINDS
GHERKINS · OLIVES
CRISPS · NUTS
```

Allow 6–7 cocktail savouries per person plus nuts and crisps.

Advance Preparations: All the dishes can be prepared beforehand.

CHEESE PASTRY

This pastry is not only used for cheese straws and other cheese biscuits, but it can be used for tiny tartlet cases instead of short crust pastry.

8 oz. flour, preferably plain · good pinch salt · shake pepper · shake cayenne pepper · pinch dry mustard · 4 oz. butter, margarine or cooking fat · 3 oz. grated Parmesan cheese · 2 egg yolks · water to mix

Sieve the dry ingredients together. Rub the butter, margarine or cooking fat into the flour. Add the cheese, then the egg yolks and sufficient water to make a rolling consistency. Roll out and use as the individual recipes. You can make a batch of pastry and use it for several recipes. Cook as the individual recipes.

CHEESE SAVOURIES

All these savouries are based upon the quantities given in the cheese pastry (above). If you are planning to entertain a number of friends make up 3 or 4 times the amount given and produce a selection of cheese savouries. These can be served with cocktails or as a savoury for a buffet or dinner party.

Cheese straws: Roll out the pastry until one-third of an inch in thickness. Cut into narrow fingers, put on to well greased baking trays. Save a little pastry to make rings. Brush straws and rings with egg white and bake for 8–10 minutes towards the top of a hot oven, 425–450°F., Gas Mark 6–7. Cool on the baking trays, then lift off carefully, store in an airtight tin. Put some of the straws through the rings to serve. Makes about 60 straws and 8–10 rings.

Savoury twists: Roll out the cheese pastry, spread half with yeast extract, top with the remaining dough. Cut into thin strips and twist. Bake as cheese straws (above). Makes about 60.

Curried patties: Roll out the pastry and cut into about 28–30 cocktail-sized rounds or 12–14 larger-sized rounds. Mince 8–10 oz. lean ham, blend with 1–2 teaspoons curry powder, 1–2 tablespoons sweet chutney, 1–2 tablespoons desiccated coconut, 1 tablespoon sultanas and a little chopped parsley. Put into the centre of the rounds. Brush the edges with water, fold over and seal the edges. Bake for 15 minutes in the centre of a moderate to moderately hot oven, 375–400°F., Gas Mark 5–6. Makes 28–30 cocktail savouries.

COCKTAIL QUICHE LORRAINE

short crust or cheese pastry (see page 70 or above) · 4–6 rashers bacon · 3 eggs · seasoning · 3 oz. grated Parmesan cheese · ¾ pint milk

Line small cocktail-sized tartlet tins with short crust or cheese pastry. The quantity of cheese pastry above lines about 36 tartlet cases. If using short crust pastry you need 10 oz. flour etc. to line the same number of tins. Fry the bacon lightly, then chop finely and divide between the tartlets. Beat the eggs with the seasoning, cheese and milk. Spoon into the uncooked pastry cases, bake for 7–8 minutes in the centre of a moderately hot to hot oven, 400–425°F., Gas Mark 5–6. Lower the heat to very moderate and set for a further 10–15 minutes. Makes about 36.

AVOCADO TARTLETS

cheese pastry (see above) · 1–2 egg whites · Filling: 2 large ripe avocado pears · 2 tablespoons lemon juice · 2 tablespoons thick mayonnaise · 2–3 tablespoons whipped cream or soft cream cheese · seasoning · Garnish: watercress

Make the pastry. Roll out thinly, cut into rounds and line

Making Cheese Pastry

36 tiny cocktail tartlet tins. Prick the base of the tarts with a fork, brush with egg white to give a shine and bake as the Cheese Straws (above). Allow to cool. Do *not* fill until just before serving. Halve the pears, remove the pulp, mash with the lemon juice and mayonnaise and blend with the cream or cream cheese, season. Spoon into the tartlet cases and top with watercress leaves. These small tartlet cases may be cooked earlier and stored until ready to fill.

To vary: Make a smaller amount of the avocado mixture, fill half the tartlet cases, then fill the rest with scrambled eggs and chopped prawns, flaked cooked or canned salmon and mayonnaise or chopped ham blended with cream cheese and mayonnaise.

MORE COCKTAIL SAVOURIES

Base for canapés: These can be rounds of buttered bread, toast, pastry, fried bread (well drained), tiny plain biscuits or rounds of cheese pastry (baked as cheese straws, page 118).

Anchovy and egg canapés: Hard boil 2 eggs, remove the yolks and mash with 2 oz. butter, anchovy essence and a shake of pepper. Pipe on to the base and top with sliced stuffed olives of pieces of cheese. *Makes 20.*

Asparagus Rolls: Spread thin slices of brown bread and butter with cream cheese or thick mayonnaise and roll round asparagus tips. If you roll the bread slices with a rolling pin they are more pliable.

Caviare Canapés: Top rounds of brown bread and butter with slices of hard boiled egg and caviare. If you blend the caviare with a little thick cream and lemon juice it is softer and easier to spread.

Cheese Bites: Cut neat pieces of slightly under-ripe Danish Blue cheese, Cheddar, Cheshire or other firm cheese. Top with pineapple pieces, then glacé or Maraschino cherries, or with grapes or halved walnuts. Put cocktail sticks through these.

Cheese Whirls: Blend Demi-sel cheese or a cream cheese spread with butter, mayonnaise or soured cream to make a piping consistency. Pipe on to the base. Sprinkle with paprika.

Christmas Menus

Most families like a traditional meal at Christmas, with turkey or goose as the main dish, followed by Christmas Pudding.

MENU

MELON OR SOUP
ROAST TURKEY WITH STUFFINGS
SAUSAGES
ROAST POTATOES
BREAD AND CRANBERRY SAUCES
CHRISTMAS PUDDING
BRANDY BUTTER
MINCE PIES
CHEESE TRAY

This menu would serve 10–12 people with plenty of turkey left over to serve cold.

Advance Preparations: Make the stuffings for the turkey (these can be frozen if wished). Prepare the crumbs for the bread sauce; this also can be frozen and so can the cranberry sauce.

Cook the Christmas pudding some weeks before Christmas. Make the brandy butter and the mince pies a day or so beforehand (although both freeze well).

ROAST TURKEY

18 lb. turkey (weight when trussed) ·
4 oz. butter or about 8 oz. fat bacon ·
Chestnut stuffing: 1 lb. chestnuts ·
½ pint ham or turkey stock · 4 oz. ham ·
8 oz. pork sausagemeat · seasoning ·
little extra stock ·
Parsley and thyme stuffing: 8 oz. soft breadcrumbs ·
3–4 tablespoons chopped parsley ·
grated rind and juice of 2 lemons ·
4 oz. shredded suet or melted margarine or butter ·
½–1 tablespoon chopped fresh thyme · seasoning ·
2 eggs

When calculating the weight of the turkey and cooking time include the weight of the stuffings as well. Put the stuffings at either end of the turkey and cover with the butter or bacon. Allow 15 minutes per lb. and 15 minutes over for a bird up to 12 lb. in weight, after this add an additional 12 minutes per

lb. up to 21 lb., after this 10 minutes only for each additional 1 lb. If the bird is exceptionally broad-breasted, allow a little extra cooking time; so the 18 lb. turkey plus the stuffings would need a total of nearly 5 hours. Set the oven to hot, 425–450°F., Gas Mark approximately 7, then after the first 30–40 minutes lower the heat to moderately hot, approximately 400°F., Gas Mark 5–6. Remember if using a covered roasting tin that you should add an additional 20 minutes' cooking time and the same thing applies if wrapping the bird in foil. Time the cooking so that the turkey comes out of the oven about 8–10 minutes before you wish to carve it; this short 'rest' allows the flesh to set a little and makes it easier to carve. Put sausages into the oven about 45 minutes before the end of the cooking time and potatoes to roast about 1 hour before the end of the cooking time.

CHESTNUT STUFFING

Slit the chestnut skins and boil in water for 5–10 minutes, then remove the skins while hot. Put the chestnuts into the stock and simmer until tender and most of the stock has been absorbed. Sieve and mix with the chopped ham, sausagemeat, seasoning and enough stock to give a moist mixture.

PARSLEY AND THYME STUFFING

Mix the breadcrumbs with the parsley, grated lemon rind, suet, margarine or butter, thyme, seasoning, lemon juice and eggs.

BREAD SAUCE

6 oz. soft white breadcrumbs · 1 pint milk ·
1 oz. butter · 1 onion (stuck with cloves if wished) ·
seasoning · 5–6 tablespoons thick cream

Put all the ingredients into a pan, bring to the boil then leave to infuse over a pan of hot water. Heat, stirring well, just before the meal and remove the onion.

CRANBERRY SAUCE

½ pint water · 4–6 oz. sugar · 1 lb. cranberries ·
4 oz. sultanas (optional) · 2 tablespoons port wine

Make a syrup of the water and sugar. Add the cranberries

The Christmas Dinner

and simmer steadily with the sultanas, if using, until tender. Sieve or emulsify to make a smooth mixture and blend with the port wine. If preferred do not sieve, but keep whole.

FEATHER-LIGHT CHRISTMAS PUDDING

12 oz. seedless raisins · 4 oz. sultanas ·
4 oz. currants · 3 tablespoons dry sherry ·
4 tablespoons orange juice · grated rind 2 oranges ·
grated rind 1 lemon · 2 tablespoons marmalade ·
6 oz. margarine or butter · 6 oz. moist brown sugar ·
3 eggs · 6 oz. soft breadcrumbs ·
6 oz. flour, plain or self-raising ·
1 teaspoon mixed spice · 2 tablespoons lemon juice

This pudding can be made several weeks before Christmas, but if you have left it until near the day, it is an excellent choice since it does not require time to mature. Put the dried fruits with the sherry and orange juice into a basin and leave for 1 hour. Cream the orange and lemon rinds, the marmalade, margarine or butter and sugar until soft. Gradually beat in the eggs, then add the crumbs, the flour sieved with the spice, and the lemon juice. Lastly add the fruit with all the moisture. Put into a 3-pint well-greased basin, press down firmly, cover with greased greaseproof paper and foil and steam for 3–4 hours. Remove the damp covers, put on dry covers and store in a cool place. Steam for 2 hours on Christmas Day.

To vary: Traditional rich dark pudding: Use another 4 oz. sultanas and another 4 oz. currants. Use stout instead of orange juice and shredded suet in place of margarine or butter. Add 4–5 oz. chopped candied peel, a small grated carrot, a small grated apple and 2–4 oz. chopped blanched almonds. Add ½–1 teaspoon ground cinnamon. Steam for 4–5 hours then a further 2–3 hours on Christmas Day.

BRANDY BUTTER (HARD SAUCE)

8 oz. unsalted butter · 1 lb. sieved icing sugar ·
up to ¼ pint brandy ·
blanched almonds and cherries (optional)

Cream the butter and sugar, then gradually work in the brandy. Pile or pipe into a dish and top with almonds and cherries, if wished. Chill well. Serves up to 16.

MINCE PIES

These can be made with short crust pastry, sweet short crust, flaky or puff pastry. Short crust pastry made with 1 lb. flour etc. will give 24–30 individual mince pies.

Roll out the pastry fairly thinly. Use just over half the pastry and cut into rounds, put these into fairly deep patty tins. Fill with mincemeat. Damp the edges of the pastry. Cut out smaller rounds with the remaining pastry, press on top of the filling. Seal the edges, make 2 slits on top to allow the steam to escape. Bake for approximately 15–20 minutes in the centre of a hot oven, 425°F., Gas Mark 6–7, until pale golden and firm. Dust with sieved icing sugar or caster sugar.

HOME-MADE MINCEMEAT

Home-made mincemeat is very easy to make. As it requires no cooking (except when put into mince pies or other dishes), do not cut down on the amount of sugar and whisky or other alcohol.

8 oz. currants ·
4 oz. seedless or stoned chopped raisins ·
4 oz. sultanas · 1 peeled, cored and grated apple ·
4 oz. brown sugar ·
4 oz. shredded suet or melted margarine or butter ·
4 oz. finely chopped candied peel ·
3 oz. finely chopped blanched almonds ·
1 teaspoon mixed spice · 1 teaspoon grated nutmeg ·
4 tablespoons whisky, brandy or rum ·
grated rind and juice of 1 lemon

Mix all the ingredients together, put into jars, seal down and keep in a cool dry place.

Suggested Drinks

As Christmas celebrations are shared by all ages it is wise to have a selection of alcoholic and soft drinks.

Roast Goose

Fresh Fruit Salad

MENU

MELON, GRAPEFRUIT OR SOUP
ROAST GOOSE WITH APPLE SAUCE
AND SAGE AND ONION STUFFING
ROAST POTATOES
CHRISTMAS PUDDING AND MINCE PIES
(see page 124)
FRESH FRUIT SALAD
CHEESE TRAY

Since goose is large-boned poultry, with little meat on the breast, a bird weighing about 12 lb. will serve only 8 people or even less.
Advance Preparations: As Menu on page 122.

ROAST GOOSE

The oven temperature is the same as for roast turkey, page 122. Do not use any form of fat over the bird. The important point is to make sure the excess fat runs out of the bird. It is quite a good idea to put the goose on a rack (or trivet) in the roasting tin or to pour away the surplus fat during cooking. Follow the timing for roast turkey on page 122. Prick the skin of the goose several times during cooking to allow the fat to 'spurt out'. Do this *lightly* – if you prick too hard there is a tendency for the fat to run *into* the flesh.

Serve roast goose, as roast turkey, with thickened gravy made by obtaining a good stock from the giblets of the bird. The recipe for apple sauce is on page 54.

SAGE AND ONION STUFFING

4 large onions · seasoning · ½ pint water ·
6 oz. soft breadcrumbs ·
½–1 tablespoon chopped sage or 1 teaspoon dried sage ·
4 oz. shredded suet or melted margarine ·
1–2 eggs (optional)

Peel and chop the onions and simmer in the well-seasoned water for 10 minutes. Strain and blend with the rest of the ingredients. Bind with an egg and stock, the 2 eggs or all onion stock. Put into the goose.

FRESH FRUIT SALAD

½ pint water · 2 oranges · 1 lemon · 3–4 oz. sugar ·
2 lb. mixed prepared fresh fruit

Put the water, with *thin* strips of orange and lemon rind, into the saucepan. Take just the top 'zest' from the fruit. Simmer for 5 minutes. Add the sugar, stir until dissolved then add the orange and lemon juice. Strain over the prepared fruit, allow to become cold.
To vary: Add a little sherry, kirsch, Cointreau or Maraschino to the syrup.
Use all fresh orange and lemon juice, omit the water and sugar.

Index

ACKNOWLEDGEMENTS

The publishers would like to acknowledge the help of the following in providing photographs for this book: National Dairy Council: Peach and Cherry Trifle page 14, Banana and Lemon Cream page 34; Pasta Foods Ltd: Mexican Frankfurters page 44; RHM Foods Ltd: Mexican Macaroni page 30; Syndication International: Cauliflower Surprise page 47, Fruit Meringue Trifle page 79, composite photographs on pages 72, 109. The publishers would like to acknowledge the help of the following for their loan of accessories for photography: Below Stairs, 212 Upper Richmond Road, London S.W. 14: fine furniture for cover photograph; Carrier Cookshops, 82 Pimlico Road, London S.W. 1: pages 17, 37, 43, 61, 65; Casa Pupo, 56 Pimlico Road, London S.W. 1: pages 23, 40, 81; Craftsmen Potters' Association, Marshall Street, London W. 1: page 53; Crocks Reject China, Richmond Bridge, Richmond, Surrey: china for cover photograph also pages 2, 3, 10, 17, 48, 49, 111; Danasco Ltd, Chelsea Manor Gardens, London S.W. 3: china for cover photograph; Elizabeth David, 46 Bourne Street, London S.W. 1: pages 31, 33; Garrard, 112 Regent Street, London W. 1: page 106; Wedgwood from Gered, Piccadilly, Regent Street, London W. 1: pages 46, 85; Heal's Ltd., 196 Tottenham Court Road, London W. 1: china for cover photograph; Robert Jackson & Co., 172 Piccadilly, London W. 1: pages 8, 21, 86, 88, 104; David Mellor Ironmonger, 4 Sloane Square, London S.W. 1: pages 20, 22, 51, 78, 101, 117 also cutlery in most of the photographs; Harvey Nichols, Knightsbridge, London S.W. 1: pages 11, 31, 38, 40, 43, 102, 103, 114; Rosenthal Studio House Ltd: 102 Brompton Road, London S.W. 1: pages 15, 39; Wilson & Gill, 37 Regent Street, London W. 1: page 99.

WEIGHTS AND MEASURES

Imperial	US
2½ oz Allbran	1 cup
1 lb apples (diced)	4 cups
2 oz bacon, streaky	3 slices fatty bacon
2 oz bean sprouts	1 cup
4 oz black or redcurrants, blueberries	1 cup
4 oz breadcrumbs (fine dried)	1 cup
2 oz breadcrumbs (fresh soft), cake crumbs	1 cup
8 oz butter, margarine, lard, dripping	1 cup butter, margarine, shortening, drippings
3-4 oz button mushrooms	1 cup
8 oz cabbage (finely chopped)	3 cups
12 oz clear honey, golden syrup, molasses, black treacle	1 cup (1 lb = 1⅓ cups) honey, maple syrup, molasses, black treacle
1 oz cooking chocolate	1 square baking chocolate
4½ oz cornflour	1 cup cornstarch
8 oz cottage, cream cheese	1 cup
¼ pint single, double cream	½ cup + 2 tablespoons (⅔ cup) light, heavy cream
2 oz curry powder	½ cup
3 oz desiccated coconut	1 cup shredded coconut
4 oz digestive biscuits (8 biscuits)	1 cup Graham crackers
7 oz dried chick peas, haricot beans	1 cup garbanzos, navy beans
4 oz flour, plain or self-raising	2 tablespoons all-purpose or self-rising flour
½ oz gelatine (1 tablespoon sets 2 cups liquid)	2 envelopes
3 oz preserved ginger (chopped)	⅓ cup
8 oz glacé cherries	1 cup candied cherries
3½ lbs gooseberries	9 cups
4 oz grated cheese, Cheddar type, Parmesan	1 cup
4 oz ground almonds	1 cup
7 oz long-grain rice	1 cup
4 oz macaroni, raw	1 cup
8 oz mashed potato	1 cup
8 oz minced raw meat	1 cup ground raw meat, firmly packed
4 oz nuts (chopped)	1 cup
2 oz onion (chopped)	½ cup
2 oz parsley (chopped)	1½ cups
6 oz pickled beetroot (chopped)	1 cup
6 oz peeled prawns	1 cup peeled shrimp
5-6 oz raisins, currants, sultanas (chopped), candied peel	1 cup (1 lb = 3 cups)
5 oz raspberries	1 cup
3½ oz rolled oats	1 cup
8 oz sausagemeat	1 cup
5 oz strawberries, whole	1 cup
8 oz sugar, castor or granulated	1 cup, firmly packed
4 oz sugar, icing (sieved)	1 cup sifted confectioner's sugar
8 oz tomatoes (chopped)	1 cup
2¾ oz (smallest can) tomato purée	¼ cup
4 teaspoons dried yeast	4 teaspoons active dry yeast
¼ pint yoghurt	½ cup + 2 tablespoons (⅔ cup)

Liquid Measurements

20 fluid oz = 1 Imperial pint	16 fluid oz = 1 American pint
10 fluid oz = ½ Imperial pint	8 fluid oz = 1 American cup